Social Stratification   **E.M. SHAW**

D0756163

THE STUDENTS LIBRARY OF SOCIOLOGY

GENERAL EDITOR : ROY EMERSON
Professor of Sociology
University of East Anglia

Social Stratification

by Carol Owen

Department of Rural Sociology
Cornell University

LONDON
ROUTLEDGE & KEGAN PAUL
NEW YORK: HUMANITIES PRESS

First published 1968
by Routledge & Kegan Paul Ltd
Broadway House, 68–74 Carter Lane
London, E.C.4

Printed in Great Britain
by Willmer Brothers Limited
Birkenhead, Cheshire

SBN 7100 6086 6 c
SBN 7100 6087 4 p

General editor's introduction

Today sociology is going through a phase of great expansion. Not only is there a widespread general interest in the subject, but there is a rapid growth in the numbers of new courses at Universities, Colleges of Further Education, and elsewhere. As a result there is an increasing number of potential readers of introductory textbooks. Some will be motivated by general interest; some will want to find out enough about the subject to see whether they would like to pursue a formal course in it; and others will already be following courses into which an element of sociology has been fused. One approach to these readers is by means of the comprehensive introductory volume giving a general coverage of the field of sociology; another is by means of a series of monographs each providing an introduction to a selected topic. Both these approaches have their advantages and disadvantages. The *Library of Sociology* adopts the second approach. It will cover a more extensive range of topics than could be dealt with in a single volume; while at the same time each volume will provide a thorough introductory treatment of any one topic. The reader who has little or no knowledge in the field will find within any particular book a foundation upon which to build, and to extend by means of the suggestions for further reading.

Social inequalities continue to be much discussed despite a tendency in polite conversation to deny that they really exist or at least to assert that they are no longer important. Very often 'class' emerges in such discussions as a very important if very loosely defined concept. But social class is only one basis for the existence of these inequalities, and Mrs. Owen discusses some alternatives such as caste, and estate. The reason for an interest in social inequality is not simply to put people into pigeonholes according to some principle of higher or lower, just for its own sake. All societies exhibit social inequalities which are woven into the pattern of social relations. By analysing these inequalities it is possible to see how different aspects of the society hang together. For instance, differences in educational opportunity, in patterns of health, and in sub-cultural value systems all appear to be related to socio-economic group in Britain.

In this book Mrs. Owen has attempted to provide an overview of this complex and wideranging topic. From her treatment it is possible for the reader to follow the complexities of social stratification over a number of examples chosen from different societies and epochs. With this as a basis, the interested reader will find in the suggestions for further reading given at the end of the book a means of developing an understanding of some of the more advanced theoretical problems in the field.

A. R. EMERSON

Contents

CONTENTS

List of Tables

Acknowledgments

The author and publisher wish to express their thanks to the following publishers and authors for permission to reprint copyrighted material:

Allen and Unwin: Lockwood, D., *The Blackcoated Worker*, 1958;

Cambridge University Press: *The Cambridge Medieval History*, planned by J. B. Bury, 1923; Hutton, J. H., *Caste in India*, 1946;

Clarendon: Stacey, M., *Tradition and Change*, 1960, by permission of the Clarendon Press, Oxford;

Controller of H.M. Stationery Office: Heady, J. A. and Heasman, M. A., *Social and Biological Factors in Infant Mortality*, 1959; Registrar General's Decennial Supplement, *Occupational Mortality*, 1958; *Higher Education*, 1963;

Gollancz: Thompson, E. P., *The Making of the English Working Class*, 1963;

Harcourt, Brace and World: Barber, B., *Social Stratification*, 1957; Wilson, L. and Kolb, W. L., *Sociological Analysis*, 1949;

International publishers: Marx, K., *Capital*, *Vol. I*, 1887;

MacGibbon and Kee: Guttsman, W. L., *The British Political Elite*, 1963;

The Macmillan Company: Davis, Kingsley, *Human Society*, New York, 1949, Copyright 1948, 1949;

Methuen and Raymond Postgate: Cole, G. D. H. and Postgate, R., *The Common People*, 1961;

Oxford University Press: Gerth, H. H. and Mills, C. W., *From Max Weber: Essays in Sociology*, 1958;

Routledge and Kegan Paul: Glass, D. V., *Social Mobility in Britain*, 1954; Hall, J. and Jones, D. C., 'Social Grading of Occupations', *British Journal of Sociology*, i (1950); Halsey, A. H. and Gardner, L., 'Selection for Secondary

Education and Achievement in Four Grammar Schools',
British Journal of Sociology, iv (1953); Kelsall, R. K.,
Higher Civil Servants in Britain, 1955; Murdoch, *History
of Japan*, Vol. III; Klein, J., *Samples from English Cultures*,
Vols. I and II, 1965;

Rutgers University Press: Diehl, C., *Byzantium: Greatness
and Decline*, 1957;

Sociological Review: Goldthorpe, J. H. and Lockwood, D.,
'Affluence and the British Class Structure', xi (1963);

St. Martin's Press Inc.: Coser, R. L., *The Family: Its
Structure and Functions*, 1964;

The Viking Press Inc.: Veblen, T., *The Theory of the Leisure
Class*, 1953.

Introduction

The biblical prescription to 'judge not lest ye be judged' has done little to eliminate what appears to be an enduring, if not endearing quality of human beings—the ability to look upon their fellows through either jaundiced or rosy spectacles. Myths and history are reservoirs of villains and heroes, men of night and men of light, the worthless and the worthy. Into which social category one is born is probably the most important factor in determining the scope of a person's life experiences in a society; whom he will meet, whom he will marry, how he will raise his children; if and for how long he will go to school, what type of school he will attend, what kind of occupation he will follow, what picture of the world he will harbour and what he will think of himself, as well as many other aspects of living.

Social stratification studies are concerned with the placement of people into social categories such as high and low, upper class, middle class and working class, 'those who count' and the rest; their placement by law, by religion, by ideology and by their own and their fellows' estimations on the basis of some one or several characteristics which they possess. Such studies are directed towards determining the structure and processes of social stratification in a society or the number of levels in the skyscraper of social respect, the qualifications needed to live on any particular level and the consequences following upon such modes of existence.

C.O.

1

Different or unequal?

Social differences

All people are not, nor are there any recorded instances that they ever have been, treated alike in the presentation of the prizes of life such as food, canoes, money, education or human dignity. As the paradox is popularly stated, all men may be born equal but some are born more equal than others. They are born more equal than others because they are born into families whose members think, speak and act differently from members of other families and some of these thoughts, words and deeds are considered to be more promising, more important to the society.

Emphasis must be placed on the fact that *some* of these differences are considered of differential benefit to the society; for, to be different is not necessarily to be unequal. Social inequality means that some social differences have been evaluated as 'better' or 'worse' so that those who possess the 'better' characteristics are more highly rewarded with money, privilege, prestige or power than are those who possess the 'worse' ones.

Factual differences and moral inequality

In the first instance, then, social stratification involves the evaluation of *particular* factual differences as better or worse to possess. In Britain, for example, differences in age are not evaluated to the extent that deferential behaviour is expected towards all the elderly as was the case noted by Yang (Coser, 1964) in pre-Communist China where

> To demonstrate the glory and prestige of age, an individual's sixtieth birthday and every subsequent tenth birthday were celebrated with a feast and ceremony as elaborate and impressive as the family and close relatives could possibly afford.

Certain qualities and actions, such as being six feet tall, voting Tory and reading the *Daily Telegraph* may be associated with superior positions, but the possession of these characteristics alone does not evoke envy or respectful behaviour. The kinds of factual differences judged to be better or worse depend upon what is highly desirable in a society and the power of various individuals and groups in that society to demand respect for their particular definitions of the good and evil things in life.

Although differences of sex and race are evaluated in our society and are thus part of the phenomenon of social inequality, these differences and their contingent consequences will not be considered here. The evaluation of sex and race differences tends to be singled out for special study largely because of the social agitation arising from such evaluations and the designation of such agitation as a social problem.

Rank order

The second characteristic of social stratification is that

3

the evaluation of particular factual differences results in a grading of the population into superior and inferior strata, all those in a single stratum sharing a roughly similar rank. For example, if education were considered a good thing to possess and the possession of more of a good thing considered even better, people would be ranked according to the number of years spent at school. Those with many years to their credit would be top-ranked and would expect and receive deference from others ranked in relation to them.

Persistence of rank orders

A third characteristic of social stratification is that a particular system of unequally evaluated ranks persists over time. For example, amongst the Blackfoot Indians of the American plains, skill in hunting, efficiency in organization and success in human relations were qualities sought after in a leader. Presumably upon the basis of these qualities a tribal chief was selected from amongst the chiefs of the bands making up the tribe. However, frequently, the tribal chief was selected from the same band and even from the same family in the same band. This persistent selection would indicate the possible presence of some kind of stratification based upon the assumption that administrative and manipulative skills were inheritable; whereas if the tribal chiefs were selected from different families in different bands with no family or band continuity in the transmission of social power, social stratification in this context would be non-existent. The characteristics 'selected' for evaluation must either *be* capable or be thought to be capable of being transmitted from generation to generation.

A brief digression is necessary here over the use of the term 'transmission' in a context other than that of genetic

4

inheritance. We speak of the inheritance of social position, money, cowardice, resignation and ambition in
the same terms as the inheritance of blue eyes, brown
hair, ten fingers, ten toes and a nervous system. The terms
are the same but the phenomena are different. Cultural
transmission depends not upon genes but upon laws,
customs, education, the setting of examples by older
people and the expectations, hopes, fears and aspirations
of parents for the young; because much of what is taught
to and observed by young people is absorbed by them
to the extent that it becomes built into their personalities.
We tend to expect from children what we have experienced from their parents and frequently, our expectations are confirmed not because of genetic regularities
but rather because of social and cultural regularities.
Many of these social and cultural regularities are
strengthened and facilitated by social stratification.

Consequences for life experiences

A fourth characteristic of social stratification is that it
has consequences in terms of opportunities for different
experiences and for the manifestation of different qualities in life for those variously located in the social skyscraper. For example, in an investigation into children's
health in Newcastle-upon-Tyne in the 1930's (McGonigle
and Kirby, 1936), Dr. J. C. Spence recorded the heights
and weights of one hundred and twenty-five children
from families where the father worked either as a
labourer or an artisan and an equivalent number of
children from families where the father worked either
in the professions or in commerce. He found that a higher
proportion of children from professional and commercial
families were above normal height and weight while a

5

B

higher proportion of children from labouring and craft families were below this standard.

In brief, then, social stratification refers to the ranking of people in terms of superiority and inferiority into a relatively stable hierarchy according to the actual or assumed possession of characteristics which are considered to be of greater or lesser social value and this ranking has consequences for the life experiences of the people thus ranked.

Evaluation

The first problem in describing a system of social stratification is to determine which characteristics are evaluated in order to see how people can be considered unequal. Theorists disagree over particular aspects of the unit to be evaluated, but many agree over the general principle that what a person does for most of his waking hours, that is, his full-time job, is the most common characteristic which is judged in terms of relative importance to the society by other members of that society. This characteristic will be called a person's functional role or the part he plays in maintaining or changing the organization of a society.

In societies where different tasks have become associated with different specialists, the functional role which is evaluated can be inferred from the occupation; hence the agreement over the evaluation of a person's *full-time* job as being of greater or lesser importance to the organization of a society. However, in those societies where each person tends to be a jack-of-all-trades, full-time occupations are few and far between, so that the highly evaluated functional role may not require the incumbent's full-time participation. In such societies respect and deference may be proffered to part-time role

6

participants as in the case of the leopard-skin chief amongst the Nuer of the Southern Sudan (Evans-Pritchard, in Fortes and Evans-Pritchard, 1948). This chief was not a chief in the sense that he could rule or command obedience or use force but his special role was to mediate in cases of cattle theft and murder between families. Aggrieved kin were not compelled to use his services in settling disputes but he was available for the purpose of peace-keeping and could become prominent in a community even though he was seldom called upon to act as a mediator. Thus, it appears to be the functional role or the part played in keeping the peace, aiding in the adjustment of fellow citizens to demands from the physical environment or from other peoples and in contributing to the achievement of common goals and a quality of life acceptable to most which is evaluated, the individual being judged according to the value placed upon his functional roles. The determination of which of the functional roles played by an individual in a society is to be considered crucial gives rise, however, to problems. Is occupation or contribution to family life or community service the all-important factor or is some special combination of these necessary to establish a person's value to the society? As yet this question has no general answer but must be asked anew in each society studied.

Ranking

It was noted earlier that the idea of a hierarchy was involved in the conception of a stratification system; therefore, if people are to be judged as more or less worthy according to their functional roles, the functional roles must be organized into some kind of rank order. With the following generalization Barber (1957) suggests two criteria for the ordering of functional roles—knowledge and responsibility:

> ... the greater the amount of knowledge or responsibility, or the two in combination, required for performance in a given role, the higher stratificational position of the incumbent of that position.

Knowledge is considered here both in terms of quantity and quality; quantity in the sense of a large number of specific facts and quality as exhibited through generalized and systematized knowledge from which specific facts can be deduced; while responsibility refers to the amount of control over and direction of other people. These two criteria have been culled from empirical work on the rating of occupations by samples of the general public and special groups such as students.[1] Thus, an electronics engineer would be rated more highly than an electrician and a theoretical physicist more highly than a high school physics teacher or an electronics engineer.

The identification of two criteria, however, raises a further problem in that there may be more than one rank order of social respect in a society, as the relationship between knowledge and responsibility is still imperfectly understood. With the use of two criteria, one rank order will be recognized to the extent that knowledge does not occur without responsibility and vice versa.

Relation of other social differences to differences in rank

Although one cannot take for granted that any specific

[1]For material on the difficulties associated with such ratings see:
CAPLOW, T., *The Sociology of Work*, McGraw Hill, New York, 1964; also in the Bibliography—Gusfield and Schwartz (1963); Hall and Jones (1950); Himmelweit, Halsey and Oppenheim (1952); and Young and Willmott (1956).

8

relationship exists in all societies, the literature abounds with examples of relationships between differences in education, income, hospital treatment, ideas, aspirations, wealth and language, to mention only a few, and differences in social rank. In Britain, for example, of a total of twenty-six million incomes noted from tax returns in 1960 eleven million of these were less than £500 per year and ½ million or 2% of the total number of incomes were greater than £2,000 per year. Do those who possess high incomes also possess high social prestige? It seems that they are more likely to than are those with low incomes; for as will be seen in Chapter Four, those occupations which are rated more highly in social prestige tend to be those which command high monetary return.

The ownership of property is also unevenly distributed throughout the population. Of all adults over twenty-five years of age in England and Wales in 1954 the richest one per cent owned 43% of the total private property and the richest ten per cent owned over 70% (Harbury, 1962). Do those who possess this high percentage of the available property also possess high social prestige? This is a difficult question to answer generally unless those who own the bulk of the nation's capital wealth are also gainfully employed, for large scale studies of social prestige have dealt only with the social grading of occupations.

Income and property ownership are only two of the social differences which appear to be related to differences in social rank in Britain. In the chapters to follow, many more will be noted.

How rank orders persist

The delineation of rank orders in a society leads to the question of the qualifications necessary for admittance to the various levels within a rank order; for while generations come and go, social inequality lingers on. This is referred to as the problem of recruitment and perhaps the most important method of recruitment is the social and cultural transmission of qualifications from parents to children mentioned above. Sometimes this involves the complete transference of a father's social credits and discredits to his children so that their social standing is a nearly exact replica of their father's; in other cases some of the qualities and performances expected of the father are transferred to the children making it easier or more difficult for them to achieve rewards officially stated to be open for competition. There is a tendency for people to expect great things from the children of great fathers. These expectations may be grounded in the belief that the potential of greatness is inherited in the genetic sense so that the children of chiefs automatically become chiefs while the children of followers remain followers, or these expectations may follow a line of least resistance based upon the hope that some greatness may rub off onto the children so that the investment required to realize the potential may be less than that necessary to reveal the worthiness of an unpolished specimen. The net result is that to a great extent a rank system is self-perpetuating, for positions in rank orders are either largely ascribed (culturally inherited) or achieved from initial, unequal ranks. In this respect the family is a very important carrier as well as instigator of social inequality.

However, the desire of many parents to give their best for their children is not the sole factor in maintaining social inequality. To what extent people agree about the justice of a particular unequal distribution of rewards (W. G. Runciman, 1966) is also relevant; for if members of a society believe that a particular kind of social inequality is fair, just or pre-ordained, they tend to oppose any alterations. Another factor lies in the economy and the level of technology, in that as long as these remain relatively static, occupational proliferation tends to be non-existent with no new jobs created opening novel avenues into higher social ranks.

Power is also a factor to be reckoned with and there are many possibilities for its exercise. Some of these consist of enforcing social inequality through physical coercion (always the most expensive form of exercising power), or through controlling channels of communication to bring about the acceptance of beliefs congenial to high ranking groups, or through the ability of members of an elite to appear efficient in resolving the problems facing a society, or through the manipulation of rewards to ensure that privileges accrue only to denizens of an inner circle. This self-perpetuating quality of a rank system is, perhaps, its most important consequence and will be explored further in later sections.

Consequences of a social rank system

The self-perpetuating quality of social stratification has already been mentioned and earlier in this chapter the association between physical stature and occupation was briefly noted. In Chapters Three to Six other differences and their consequences will be discussed. Because of this self-perpetuating nature, phenomena labelled 'social differences' for one generation may reappear in the succeeding generation and be labelled 'consequences'.

Change in social rank systems

Although a particular system of social inequality may appear to be permanent to those enmeshed, changes do occur; changes in the composition of social ranks, for example, as in the case of cabinet ministers, a section of the political elite, during the period 1886 to 1955, documented by Guttsman (1963). From 1886 to 1916 the fathers of about 45% of cabinet ministers were landowners; sons of landowners thus constituting the largest single group of ministers, while about 3% of cabinet ministers came from families where the father was a manual worker. From 1916 to 1955 the composition of cabinet ministers in relation to fathers' occupation was altered to the extent that the fathers of about 32% were evenly divided between landowners and manual workers.

A change in the composition of elite groups may indicate a change in the channels leading to privileged positions when, for example, a cabinet position results from a trade union career rather than from a public school education. Changes in composition and in channels leading to privileged positions are referred to as recruitment changes.

A change can also occur in the number of strata visible as when one social level is further subdivided, as seen in the Indian caste system. Such a change may alter the shape of a system, although change in shape can occur with a constant number of strata (see Chapter Five). 'Shape' refers to the proportion of the population at each social level; and the shape of the British occupation system in 1949 (Glass, 1954) was a distorted diamond-shaped structure with little more than 2% of the population at the top level, but, significantly, less than 10% at the bottom level.

Another form of change is in the magnitude of the differences in rewards between various strata. For example, in industrial societies the disparities in rewards between the highest and the lowest appear greater to an outsider than those between a Blackfoot tribal chief and his people, but perhaps somewhat less than those between an Oriental despot and his peasant serfs.

Changes in beliefs can occur in a society which may have profound effects upon the arrangement and composition of social strata. For example, in the Soviet Union during the first quarter of this century the qualification essential for access to positions commanding respect changed from a 'divine right' monopolized by the nobility to a guardianship of the interests of the 'toilers of town and country' monopolized by members of the Communist Party. Beliefs relating to vertical social mobility (movement up and down the social ladder) also may contribute to alterations in the composition and relative positions of social strata as when ideas of the possibility of individual social mobility are generated in a society previously admitting only to group mobility and vice versa.

It is rare for all of these problems connected with rank orders, their persistence and alteration, to be dealt with in any single piece of research, so that large areas of ignorance relating to specific systems of social stratification exist and no frontier is considered closed.

Types of social stratification

Various terms have been used to refer to different types of social stratification but the three most commonly encountered are caste, estate and class. These are differentiated by recruitment rules and consequences, or, to put it another way, the placement of people in social strata, the ease or difficulty of moving from one stratum to another within the system and the range of privileges associated with stratum placement.

Caste

In a caste system admittance to social strata was determined by birth. The social distance between castes was maintained and emphasized by ritual observances related to ideas concerning pollution and purity, and castes were ranked in a hierarchy considered to be divinely ordained. Individual mobility from caste to caste was inconceivable in one's lifetime but an entire caste might improve its position in the social hierarchy through strict adherence to practices intended to improve ritual purity. It was in India that the most complete example of a caste system existed; however, in other societies some groups have appeared caste-like, as, for example, the Negroes in the American south.

Birth into a caste determined what foods to eat, with whom to have physical contact without endangering one's purity, how to dress, how to speak, how to conduct oneself in public, what occupation to follow and circumscribed the choice of marriage partners as well as determining many other ways of acting and thinking.

Estate

Strata in an estate system were also clearly separated from each other through legal and customary means and formed a hierarchy of three or four levels, considered in Europe to be divinely ordained; the military aristocracy or nobility, the clergy (whose leaders were ranked equally with the nobility), the merchants and artisans and the free and unfree peasants. Individual mobility from estate to estate was infrequent but not prohibited by law or custom. For example, in feudal Europe a commoner could acquire lands and a title by performing an outstanding service for the monarch or could improve his rank through entrance into the priesthood.

Birth into an estate largely determined one's general occupational field rather than one's specific job as in a caste system. It largely determined one's dress, speech and marriage choice amongst other things, but clearly formulated ideas of ritual pollution through contact were missing as were explicit prohibitions on individual mobility and marriage outside one's estate. However, there were no provisions for an estate to raise its social rank relative to other estates, so that an estate system was more open to changes in rank by individuals while being more restrictive in terms of group changes relative to a caste system.

Class

The term 'class' has had ascribed to it several meanings and tends to be applied to any stratification system which is neither of the caste or estate variety. Class will be used here in its economic sense to refer to those with similar income from similar sources who exercise similar control over their work situation and who experience similar chances for occupational mobility and standards of living in so far as such standards are dependent upon size and source of income. As an economically based category, class does not involve judgments of 'better' and 'worse'; but in our society where desirable ways of living may depend to a large extent upon the monetary reward for services rendered, some class situations are more favourable than others as means of attaining social honour or social status.

A class system is generally found in association with official beliefs in political and moral equality. Class boundaries are not defined in law or religious doctrine and marriage across class lines, although informally discouraged, is not legally or ritually banned. In theory each person in a class-stratified society is able to improve his class position in his own lifetime through his own efforts, but in practice, only limited social mobility occurs. Birth into a class usually means that a person will have particular social influences playing upon him which will facilitate or inhibit any improvement in social rank which theoretically would result from his own efforts.

Summary

Social inequality is a persistent and pervasive feature of human society involving the evaluation of various qualities and actions of individuals. Provided these evaluated qualities and actions can be perpetuated by social and cultural transmission from any older generation to any younger one, relatively stable strata composed of people of equal rank can be discerned. This stabilization of social inequality is referred to as social stratification. A stratified society will exhibit rank orders which persist over time and are associated with many differences in the life experiences of the people of that society.

Because of the diffuse nature of factors associated with social stratification, the field of inquiry is vast. The main problems posed will be considered in terms of the social differences related to rank differences and some consequences of and changes in these relationships.

2

Theories of social stratification

Although there is much descriptive material on social stratification in specific societies, the theories to organize these facts and make them meaningful are still elusive. Many writers have produced stimulating ideas which have resulted in new perspectives on the problem but few have examined systematically all the facets of social stratification. In many cases their interests have been less in describing and explaining social inequality and more in relating this to other phenomena such as attitudes and beliefs, group formation, the exercise of political power and social change, so that they have approached social stratification in an oblique way. For example, Marx's ideas on social strata are more easily comprehended in the light of his concern with evolutionary and revolutionary change. Consequently, contributions to a more general consideration of social stratification are scattered throughout the works of many writers.

From the many, a few have been chosen; Karl Marx, Max Weber, Thorstein Veblen and some contributors to the functional approach to stratification. A different selection could have been made but from these works it will be possible to discuss briefly ideas on social inequality in terms of (1) initiating conditions, (2) consequences in the sense of opportunities for life experiences and (3) changes. Extensive criticisms of these ideas can be found through the suggested readings.

Karl Marx 1818–1883

The name of Karl Marx is linked, amongst other things, with social change on a grand scale, the evolution of societies. In this evolutionary process the most important motive force, Marx considered, was the way a man made his living. As man must eat to live, argued Marx, how he gets his living will mould his mind and with this basic assumption he spent his life trying to prove the applicability of his theory of social change.

In Marx's view, social inequality did not exist in man's 'natural' state because of the common control of resources, allegedly characterized by the ownership of land by the total community with individual rights in tools, cultivation and the distribution of products. Those who laboured owned the land they laboured on, the requisite tools, their own labour-power and had rights in common over the distribution of products. When any of these factors was altered so that only some men in a society owned land or tools or rights to dispose of products or labour-power itself, social inequality was born. Which of these forms of property was alienated put a stamp on historical conditions and respectively characterized particular epochs. Precipitating factors for the alienation of property were said to be war and conquest, population growth, trade, the widening of external relations or the growth of material wants within a community; for each of these required a different division of labour if the society was to survive under the new conditions. For Marx, the term 'division of labour' did not refer to people doing different jobs like weaving or farming but to people doing different types of jobs like labouring and managing based upon the alienation of property. The 'real' division of labour was that between material and mental labour— the '. . . development in a man of one single faculty at the expense of all other faculties . . .' (1961).

This qualitative difference in property owned, or this division between material and mental labour, over-shadowed any quantitative differences; the division being seen most clearly in capitalist society. Because pro-letarians owned no tools or other means of production such as raw materials, capital or natural resources, it was always necessary for them to sell their property, their labour-power, in order to live; whereas the bour-geoisie in using their property, capital, accumulated more property in the form of profit—hence the term 'capitalist society'. This was a one-way process, for as the labour-power of the proletariat accumulated more property for the bourgeoisie, the wages of the workers remained con-stant, at best, or even declined. To extract more labour-power than required for the subsistence of the worker and to expropriate the products of this surplus labour-power was the situation of exploitation.

The life chances of those in different class situations differed dramatically, because a major consequence of owning qualitatively different property was a repetition of this unequal distribution in opportunities for acquiring other privileges. Given a favoured position in the organi-sation of economic activities, all other privileges auto-matically followed. The bourgeoisie acquired political power, favourable laws and control over the arts and sciences, while the lot of the proletariat grew worse with the progress of capitalism. All benefits accrued to capitalists, none to proletarians.

Another major consequence of owning qualitatively different property and thus occupying different class positions was said to be the development of class consciousness. Marx believed in a 'natural' economic rationality of man with the result that he thought that all those in the same class situation would come to think alike, to have the same ideas and aspirations and would work towards the same kind of society. As the economic relations of the bourgeoisie and proletariat constituted exploitation, the consciousness of each class would involve conflicting goals for the society; and as exploitation rested upon the ownership of qualitatively different property, this situation could be altered only through a major social upheaval. This major social upheaval was a consequence of the system, for the time would come when the pursuit of capital would no longer provide for the basic needs of the people; and the proletariat, bearing new techniques of production, techniques which would increase man's power over nature, would triumph when the will to revolt and the conditions for revolution coincided. In this way new epochs would be born because 'The history of all hitherto existing societies is the history of class struggles' (Marx and Engels, 1934).

Max Weber (1864–1920)

While Weber did not deny the importance of economic factors, he was not prepared to accept that man acted for bread alone, and he organized much of his work to show that other factors were important influences. Perhaps his most famous work in this line was *The Protestant Ethic and the Spirit of Capitalism*. His contribution to social stratification studies lies less in the exposition of a theory and more in the form of a clarification of issues, a guide to research and an expressed conviction that the complexity of social life required more than a monocausal explanation for all consequences.

The only hint Weber gave as to the beginnings of social inequality was that it resulted from usurpation; political, economic or psychological. When a society was faced by any of the precipitating factors suggested by Marx, an elevated social position could come about as a result of the seizing of political power, or of property or through good publicity. It would matter little to the social standing of an individual or group if they solved the problems faced by a society but it would matter a great deal that they were *seen* to do so.

Social inequality in a society could be observed by noting the 'life chances' of individuals, or the power a person had to obtain '. . . a supply of goods, external living conditions and personal life experiences . . .' (Gerth and Mills, 1958), as these chances were associated with two characteristics. The first of these was called class status, or economic position, that is, the typical opportunities a person had in life in so far as these were dependent on

> . . . the amount and kind of power, or lack of such to dispose of goods or skills for the sake of income in a given economic order. (Gerth and Mills, 1958)

The second characteristic relevant to life chances was called social status, defined as the effective claim to positive or negative privilege with respect to social prestige in so far as such a claim rested upon the excellence attributed to a mode of living, education, birth or occupation. The 'status situation' of individuals involved every aspect of one's life chances which was determined by a social judgment of honour. How a group made a claim

21

to social honour which was accepted by others was not elaborated by Weber apart from his general example of usurpation but, as will be seen below, Veblen had something to add to this.

The general consequences of occupying a privileged position were seen in terms of opportunities for future gain. For example, members of a highly privileged class could augment their life chances by policies such as price-fixing and land monopolies; they could improve their chances for high social honour by monopolizing the purchase of luxury goods and socially advantageous education thus securing a distinctive style of life. Privileged status groups could improve their economic chances in several ways, for example, by attaining preferential opportunities and eventually monopolies for well-paid positions such as high office in the civil service. Securing legal privileges such as immunity granted to a nobility could enhance their opportunities in other spheres.

Weber did not assume that possession of property brought social honour as a necessary consequence or that high income and high prestige were always found together but suggested that money and honour might be in sharp opposition—witness the trials and tribulations of the *nouveaux riches*. It was not a one-way process as Marx had insisted but each society would have to be examined in order to find the conditions under which the acquisition of privileges went from property to prestige or from prestige to property and for which groups it did so.

In Weber's view any system of social inequality needed both material and moral support. Power, to be sustained, required a legitimate basis so that in order that some might command, there would be others who could be counted on to obey. For a particular style of life to be imbued with social honour those practising this style must claim the honour but there must be others to accept such a claim. A group claiming honour could, if successful, stabilise their economic or political power of life and death so that not only would others obey but they would obey willingly with the personal belief that they were not being badly treated.

Weber's ideas about how a system of social inequality could change were intrinsically similar to those of Marx but with more stress laid upon psychological factors. If, in times of stiff economic competition, the gentry clung to traditional land use practices with the consequence of impoverishment, their economic position would be surpassed by successful innovators. High social honour might be threatened by 'technological repercussion and economic transformation' which required forms of labour not hitherto defined as honorific but which political authorities were prepared to reward.

Thorstein Veblen (1857–1929)

As an appendix to Weber's discussion of social status groups, Thorstein Veblen (1953) has left a plausible account of the basis for the social honour of a particular group in the United States—the leisure class. It should be borne in mind that he was referring to a particular group at a particular time in his descriptive accounts, but that much of what he said may be found to be applicable to many successful appropriators of social honour.

Veblen suggested that the emergence of a leisure class as a more or less permanent group in society depended on two conditions: firstly, that war or some other predatory pursuit should be an habitual way of life on the assumption that more esteem was showered on those who gathered in prizes adventitiously than on those who consistently and uneventfully shaped what was available; and secondly, that the techniques of supplying food should be at a level consistent with the abstention of some part of the population from regular work. In the course of raids and wars, booty was seized to serve as trophies or symbols of success, women apparently being one of the earliest forms of symbol. Captive females were the property of a successful predator and the goods which their industry produced also came to be appropriated; thus, claimed Veblen, was instituted the individual ownership of property. When a more peaceable way of life characterized by industrial rather than predatory activity became common, accumulated property was then taken as a symbol for predatory success, and as the opportunities for predatory activities decreased, wealth became intrinsically honourable and, therefore, necessary to one's self respect. Once wealth of itself could bestow self respect, the purpose of accumulation shifted from subsistence and consumption to the emulation of the wealthy in the form of conspicuous consumption. Thus, not only must the wealthy to maintain their honour *not* work but also they must be *seen* not to work. Veblen thought that in his time this consumption of time non-productively was characterized by

> ... the knowledge of the dead languages and the occult sciences; of correct spelling; of syntax and prosody; of the various forms of domestic music and other household art; of the latest proprieties of dress, furniture, and equipage; of games, sports and fancybred animals, such as dogs and race-horses ... manners and breeding, polite usage, decorum, and formal and ceremonial observances generally.

The functional approach

The functional approach to social stratification, generally associated with Kingsley Davis and Wilbert E. Moore (1949) although they have had many predecessors and have many successors, is the present source of stimulation for research into, and heated controversy over, social inequality. The basic proposition is that no society is classless or unstratified because of the functional necessity of stratification: that is, no society can survive without social stratification, therefore, all surviving societies exhibit social stratification. Societal survival is said to be impossible without two requirements: the necessity

> ... to instill in the proper individuals the desire to fill certain positions, and, once in these positions, the desire to perform the duties attached to them. (Davis and Moore, 1949)

These necessary motivations are provided by unequal rewards; more for filling important positions, less for filling relatively unimportant ones; the former being defined as those which are unique or which have other positions dependent upon them (key positions), all seen in relation to societal survival. Such positions carry high rank and are highly rewarded particularly if the talents required for such positions are scarce by virtue of being rare or costly and lengthy to produce. Consequently, it is necessary to influence people to work for such positions.

In the face of external or internal threats such as competition from other societies or conquest or internal conditions producing an economic surplus, it is possible for some members of a society to claim larger shares of available rewards such as goods or privileges in productive work in recognition of their subsequently greater contribution to the survival of the society—should they be successful. This greater contribution as regards protection from natural and supernatural forces is recognised by the people and the claim for unequal shares is accepted.

Social stratification is recognized in a society through graded hierarchies of rank which differ in each society depending upon the internal and external conditions faced by each society. However, there are a limited number of general functions necessary to the survival of each society: religion, government, production of wealth, administration of property, labour, technical knowledge and reproduction; and which of these will be valued above others depends upon the predominant functional problem facing the society (Parsons, in Bendix and Lipset, 1953). Those positions through which the dominant value may be implemented will be ranked higher than others and consequently, will be more highly rewarded.

As seen by the functionalists, the consequences for those occupying unequally evaluated positions are similar to those outlined by other writers. Privilege is said to breed privilege but to degrees varying from a 'closed' to an 'open' system or from a pure caste to a pure class system. However, if social power is used to consolidate privileged positions thus contravening the value of the best person for the job and if performance is unsatisfactory, there may be strains towards greater equity in rewards or recruitment policies for privileged positions.

Summary

As will be seen, none of these theories is adequate although each provides clues and insights for research. The plenitude of descriptive material on systems of social stratification is far more evident than the power of theories to explain them. A Marxian analysis fails when economic power does not bring political power and social prestige as a matter of course and is too dependent upon the motive force of man's rationality in economic affairs. Weber pointed out several deficiencies in Marx without putting forward a coherent theory of his own. The functional approach poses many serious problems. It is alleged that by adequate motivation the 'right' people can be recruited to fill functionally important positions, yet information is absent concerning the distribution of socially desirable traits in infants. The implication that but for the illegitimate usurpation of access to positions of high prestige by some parents, those most qualified (innately?) would achieve high prestige, ignores the actual practices of members of status groups. Even as an ideal model to be measured against reality, it is inapplicable largely because the original conditions for constructing the model cannot be achieved—that is, a society which did not endure because there was no social stratification, and the discovery of the distribution of socially valuable characteristics in a population untainted by social influences; not to mention the difficulty of assessing the relative dominance of functional problems (Tumin with Feldman, 1961). In the descriptive sections which follow, students may find that some of the facts conform to various aspects of theories but they will also find that many still stand in isolation.

3

Stratification in pre-industrial societies

If social stratification is taken to imply the unequal distribution of wealth in a population, then it is generally accepted that the material conditions for social stratification did not exist before the Upper Paleolithic period, the late Old Stone Age from about 25,000 to 12,000 years ago during which superior cutting tools appeared. To some extent these improved a group's chances for survival in that they were great aids in hunting. However, it is even more likely that social stratification in this context had to wait for developments such as the domestication of livestock and sedentary farming during the latter part of the period from 12,000 to 6,000 years ago, dubbed the Neolithic or New Stone Age. These advances in technology helped to relieve the never-ending search for food and shelter, in which no man, woman or child could be spared for very long, and they could have been partly responsible for the creation of an economic surplus, larger shares of which could have been claimed by priests and war leaders in recognition of services rendered or by political leaders as incarnations of the whole community.

Although there is no evidence one way or another, it seems unlikely that wealth was not only the sole reward but also the only basis for the differential evaluation of men's actions, as suggested in ideas stating the necessity for stratification of a level of technology making possible an economic surplus. Such ideas tend to presuppose an unequal distribution of prestige or power so that when an economic surplus was available, certain persons or groups in a society could not only claim the first surplus but could *continue* to claim the surpluses which *continued* to be created, this being a case of the extension of social inequality into the economic sector of life.

In an ethnically homogeneous society with a simple level of technology, people could be evaluated by the age they had achieved, the secrets they possessed or the political power they wielded without these being rewarded through economic wealth. They could be judged better or worse because of lineage or clan membership without any precondition of a level of technology sufficient to produce an economic surplus. Also, social inequality could have been externally imposed as a result of conquest or internally generated in ways as yet obscure. In some East African societies internal differentiation into superior and subordinate positions seemed to to have been furthered by a voluntary serfdom or clientship whereby weak individuals accepted economic burdens and inferior social positions in exchange for protection (Mair, 1962).

Social superiority can be achieved without dependence on wealth, although if unequal distributions of wealth are possible, a superior position may well be buttressed by wealth. As yet no general statements are adequate concerning the necessary and sufficient conditions for the development of social stratification in a society. A reason-

29

able approach to the matter is through the structural principles or values of a society as they are observed to be implemented through various roles in that society. This is only an approach to the problem, for vital questions have still to be answered—which principles become dominant in which society and how.

Hereditary rank

Although we are accustomed to thinking that hereditary ranks are synonymous with social strata, this is not always the case, as some units of the rank system may be individual positions rather than groups of positions, a case in point being the Nootka (Drucker, 1951) along the northwest coast of North America. Nootkans were divided into chiefs, commoners and slaves, the chiefs fitting into a comprehensive series of graded positions, one for each member of the group. These grades were distributed according to birth order in individual families and assumed birth order of the founders of each lineage—the first-born in the oldest family in the oldest lineage receiving the highest rank and so on down the line. That these ranks were on an individual rather than a group basis was clearly expressed through the 'potlatch' (a lavish ceremonial feast and distribution of gifts). Potlatch gifts were given out in strict accordance with rank, the rank of each receiver and his gift being publicly announced; so that if two people were of equal rank, the public announcements would have had to be made simultaneously. Nootka people have related with some dismay the events during an occasion when this was necessary and from all appearances it was a traumatic experience.

The commoners seemed to occupy a similar position *vis-à-vis* each other; each was dependent upon his chief for the necessities of life, for the use of property such as land for raising food, and water in which to catch fish, for commoners had no property rights. In return, the commoner gave his chief labour services and first fruits. Should a commoner 'have a supernatural experience' with a remote ancestor (the way in which ritual privileges were acquired), he had to give this experience, in the form of a song, to his chief as he was not allowed to participate in any ceremonial in which this song could be sung.

Ceremonial rights brought high prestige and the first born were the first served, implying some belief in a hereditary charisma, some extraordinary quality of excellence, the strength of which diminished with distance from the source. Each lineage was graded according to the length of time it had existed and within each lineage individuals were graded according to the closeness of their relationship to the founding father through order of birth.

Hereditary strata

Through the idea of the intrinsic social superiority of certain people, the Trobriand Islanders of Melanesia also have exhibited social inequality derived primarily from clan membership; but here, clans and sub-clans appeared to constitute strata, for they cut across both local and political divisions. The district of Kiriwina, for example, contained four great clans each with different grades of prestige. An explanation for the different prestige-loadings of these clans is not possible as the Trobrianders had no written history; but the islanders related myths (Malinowski, 1948) which served for them both as explanations and justifications for this state of affairs. The Trobrianders believed that the world was populated by people from underground where life went on just as it did on earth. These underground people lived in villages, recognised clans and distinctions in rank and owned property. At various points on the island they were thought to have emerged from holes or rocks or clumps of trees bearing with them their ways of life. From one such hole on Kiriwina, representatives or totem animals of the four main clans were said to have come forth from underground. First one up was the iguana, totem animal of the Lukulabuta clan, who scratched round, climbed a tree and watched. Second up was the dog, totem of the Lukuba clan which was said to have been the top clan originally. Third came the pig, totem of the Malasi clan which eventually ranked higher than the Lukuba, followed by the crocodile, totem of the Lukwasisiga, the lowest-ranking clan. The dog and the pig ran round until the dog, seeing the fruit of the noke plant, nosed it and ate it. When the pig saw this, he said, 'Thou eatest *noku*, thou eatest dirt; thou art a low-bred, a commoner: the chief, the *guya'u*, shall be I.' Ever since then the Malasi clan has been the highest ranking and the highest ranking sub-clan within the Malasi has produced the practising chiefs. The clans were ranked, the sub-clans within each clan were ranked and their privileges were buttressed by similar myths concerning ancestors from underground who brought with them various insignia of hereditary dignity, economic monopolies and special knowledge.

The rank of an individual *vis-à-vis* another individual depended upon membership in a major clan, in a sub-clan, in a lineage and, sometimes, even in a village, so that stratum affiliation shifted depending upon which of these ranks was relevant in any particular situation. Clans were homogeneous only with respect to other clans; and in activities involving clan participation strict accounts of services rendered and payments received were kept by each sub-clan and by each individual within each sub-clan.

This stratification has been likened to both the caste and class types but it is significantly different from each of these. In a caste system occupations were inherited on a group basis while amongst the Trobrianders, largely because of the narrow range of occupations, these were individually inherited. For example, in each village there was a garden magician who inherited his position and special knowledge from his mother's brother. In a class system as well as in a caste system all family members are accorded the same social rank; but amongst the Trobrianders there were always two ranks in each house as the husband had to be of a different sub-clan from the wife. If a woman of high rank married a man of lower rank, she did not assume his lowly status but was still entitled to the differential respect and treatment associated with her rank. Therefore, although the sub-clans did constitute strata for some purposes, this form of social stratification does not fit under any of the three major categories of estate, caste or class.

Social rank was gained through clan membership and based upon a 'divine' order of clans; but whether clans, sub-clans or lineages constituted strata depended upon the kind of social activity entered into. This divine order of clans did not appear to be calculated upon the degree of closeness of relationships to a single ancestress (see the myth of origin in which the order of appearance of the four totem animals was not associated with the hierarchy of rank), but there was some idea concerning the inheritance of a spiritual force which qualified people for the performance of important duties so that commoners would have faith in their performance.

The ruled and their rulers

In his book, *Oriental Despotism* (1957), Karl Wittfogel has focused on the derivation of rank from political power attained either through conquest of territories and their denizens or through control over a vital element in life—water. In these societies social rank was dependent upon one's position within the power hierarchy which was itself dependent upon the despot's whim. In Wittfogel's view there were only two effective classes, the rulers and the ruled, for any association with the power hierarchy presented golden opportunities. With the exception of the kinsmen of the king, rank and administrative office coincided; the topmost rank consisting of the ruler and his court. The ruler was an absolute autocrat who could do both good and evil whenever and however he wished. Those who were permanently ensconced in his palace, his relatives, servants, courtiers and favourites, had more opportunities than others to influence him; consequently, their prestige was considerable amongst other grades of rulers and ranks of people.

Such a system as Wittfogel has described was exemplified by the Byzantine Empire where the Imperator, the Basileus, legitimate heir of the Roman Caesars, was the supreme warlord, spiritual head and the living, breathing, walking incarnation of the law. He was unimpeachable and infallible. He nominated bishops and appointed and dismissed officials at will. As a manifestation of his temporal and spiritual glory he lived in magnificent splendour. However, the emperor was not totally indestructible, for of the one hundred and seven Byzantine emperors between 392 and 1453, only thirty-four died in bed. As one authority has put it (Diehl, 1923), '... imperial power in Byzantine was an autocracy tempered by revolution and assassination'.

The many dignitaries and officials held their positions through the grace and favour of the emperor and promotion depended upon his personal wishes. By the end of the ninth century the empire was organised into twenty-five districts or themes, each administered by a general whose salary came from local taxes but whose authority depended upon the emperor. Consistent with his total submission to the emperor, a theme ruler was like a vice-emperor except that some of the officials on his patch were directly responsible to the emperor and, therefore, well placed to report back any subversion. Other government officials extended the political control of the emperor to every aspect of town and country life —trade, religion, land ownership and morals.

For the most part the non-ruling city dwellers lived a rather squalid existence in overcrowded conditions and were fed on government bread, wine and oil. The merchants, moneylenders and bankers enjoyed a slightly more exalted position than other non-rulers but even they were in constant danger of impoverishment by some government official and suffered government overseers of their activities, as Diehl (1957) has noted, 'The State fixed the quantity of purchases, the quality of manufacture, prices and wage-rates'. The annual revenue from market and customs dues and shop rents provided a more than tidy sum for the emperor.

> It has been calculated that in the twelfth century, in Constantinople alone, shop rents and market and customs duties together furnished the Emperor with a sum of 7,300,000 gold besants, or about twenty million gold dollars,

a sum estimated about as the equivalent of what it cost to run the Empire for one day.

In the countryside some families became powerful by

extending their landholdings and this power was further increased by the bestowal of high office, salaries and endowments by the central government as premature rewards for future submission. However, the result was that in time they came to constitute a serious threat to the emperor. Landless and weak peasants compromised their personal freedom for a longer life expectancy through protection by the powerful, so that in the later stages of the empire, despotism and feudalism existed side by side.

The feudal state

This coincidence of despotism and feudalism was somewhat similar to conditions in Japan from 1192 to 1867 with the very important exception that the fortunes of the central government were less spectacular than those of the feudal lords. In theory the divine, all-powerful emperor was the absolute ruler, but in practice, the feudal lord with the most successful sword was at the apex of political power.

The relative tranquillity when one family would gain ascendancy was short-lived; and persistent, endemic warfare between land-hungry warriors destroyed much of the countryside while an impotent central administration looked on. Some of the landlords, having seen where their salvation lay, recruited landless peasants and lordless samurai and promised protection in return for allegiance and thus were able to develop their estates into viable concerns and effective supports for future military campaigns, for it was through military expertise that a family acquired power and social honour. With few exceptions the emperor sanctioned this *de facto* power by bestowing upon the victor the title of Shogun (a shortened form of the term which literally meant 'barbarian-subduing generalissimo') which came to refer to the actual head of the ruling family. It was a military feudalism within a legal and hereditary stratification system

This system was composed of four ranks: warriors, farmers, artisans and merchants; each of which was further subdivided, and movement between them was possible but difficult, their relative positions being expressed in legal as well as traditional forms. An indication of the high prestige of the warrior or samurai rank comes from a document referred to as the Legacy of Iyeyasu (Kennedy, 1963), the founder of the Tokugawa Shogunate:

> The *samurai* are the masters of the four classes. Agriculturalists, artisans and merchants may not behave in a rude manner towards *samurai*. The term for a rude man is 'other than expected fellow'; and a *samurai* is not to be interfered with in cutting down a fellow who has behaved to him in a manner other than is expected.

The code of conduct for the samurai was strict and made their honour dependent upon total loyalty to their respective lords in return for which the lords rewarded them with food, money and in times of peace, administrative positions.

Power and style of life, not wealth, brought prestige and rank (merchants were low men on the totem pole) and this power was attained by military exploit, made possible by the ownership of land administered by loyal vassals and by peasants and artisans who pledged their labour in return for protection. Individuals could alter their rank within an estate and in some cases could effect entrance into a higher estate, for example, through adoption into a warrior family or personal service to a lord.

This latter possibility was a major differentiating factor between an estate and a caste system of stratification, for individuals could alter the esteem which others accorded to them but they could never alter their caste.

Caste

The most thorough-going system of caste stratification known was that in India. According to Hindu religious doctrine as quoted by Hutton (1946), four *varna*[1] were divinely created; '. . . . the Brahman who sprang from the mouth of the deity, the Kshatriya who was created from his arms, the Vaishya who was formed from his thighs, and the Sudra who was born from his feet'. The Brahmans were charged with the obligation to uphold and guide the social order by serving as priests and teachers of sacred knowledge, the Kshatriyas with providing military protection and ruling in accordance with religious doctrine, the Vaishyas with the obligation to be productive and the Sudras to serve the other three through manual labour and menial tasks and to do so peaceably. The relative positions of the four varna were fixed by religious doctrine and traditional law, and ideas of ritual purity acted as a chasm between the top three strata and the Sudras. To touch a low-caste or anything touched by one brought ritual pollution. Kingsley Davis (1949) has summarised the main criteria for delineating an 'unclean' caste:

(1) Inability to be served by clean Brahmins,
(2) Inability to be served by barbers, water-carriers, tailors, etc. who serve the caste Hindus,

[1] *Varna* is a rather indeterminate expression at times referring to colour or points of the compass but generally to groups of castes.

(3) Limitation on contact with caste Hindus because of possible pollution,

(4) Inability to serve water to caste Hindus,

(5) Inability to use public conveniences such as roads, ferries, wells, or schools,

(6) Inability to enter Hindu temples,

(7) Inability to dissociate oneself from a despised occupation.

There have been many explanations put forward for the existence of the caste system in India and nowhere else, the traditional one serving as a myth of origin (Hutton, 1946). Non-traditional explanations have included 'a clever plot devised by the priesthood to consolidate its position', a community of interest based upon occupation or a kind of guild formation, an attempt to keep occupational secrets in the family, the association of race with function, and many others. One of the more plausible theories takes account of food taboos and ideas of mana (a term referring to a spiritual force possessed to some degree by each individual, persons of higher rank possessing more) associated with ritual pollution characteristic of exclusive tribal groups. It was postulated that the Aryan invaders, themselves internally differentiated by rank, maintained their social distance from the conquered by building and capitalizing on these taboos. In time the exclusive tribal groups were drawn into a comprehensive stratification system sanctioned by a religious and magical doctrine of pollution, at first through food and later through contact. However, the origins of the Indian caste system are still far from clear.

A caste was a social group, membership of which was hereditary and fixed for life (except for the possibility of becoming outcaste) and whose members were constrained to marry within the major caste but outside their own clan and lineage subdivisions. Each major caste was subdivided; each subdivision was frequently subdivided and so on, almost *ad infinitum*, each subdivision being treated as a caste with its own strict rules concerning food preparation, eating, drinking, smoking, bodily contact, spatial proximity to members of other castes, the wearing of ornaments, language and occupation, to mention a few. Previous to the Second World War, Hutton has said that there were about 3,000 castes, but how many effective subdivisions of these there were, one does not know. One cannot do justice to the complexity of caste organization in India in such a short space, for each subdivision had its own caste restriction for interfering with '... all the relations and events of life, and with what precedes and follows ... life'.

Summary

From these few brief examples, it can be seen that the differential possession of wealth was not the sole determinant of social rank nor was it the only reward for services rendered nor did its possession automatically bring further privileges. It seems unlikely then that the generation of social stratification depended entirely upon a level of technology sufficient to create an economic surplus as has been suggested by Herskovits (1952) amongst others. The evidence from pre-industrial societies seems to support the approach that positions in a society carry different prestige-loadings according to the value attached to the actions and purposes subsumed in the position.

We have seen that an important principle of stratification was the first-born or first-arrived. Amongst the Nootka this principle was applied to clans, sub-clans, lineages and individuals and manifested through potlatch rights. This principle was also in evidence in East Africa where 'This kind of social prestige, based on first arrival in a vicinity, is reciprocally recognized from place to place'.[2] Amongst the Trobrianders this principle seemed to have been superseded by some idea of ritual pollution for although all the clans were believed to have arrived at the same time, representatives of two of the clans were passive while a third blotted his copybook right from the start thus losing his superiority.

Political power and military prowess were also important for the derivation of social rank, this being especially pointed in the case of feudal Japan where merchants constituted the last estate. The positions which were considered important to the welfare of a society were those which were accorded high prestige, but vital problems remain to be solved: *which* positions are considered important to the welfare of a society, by whom are they so considered and how did this come about? We may find that in many cases, a successful claim to social prestige is a colossal confidence game.

[2] I am indebted to Dr. Douglas for pointing out the importance of this principle. Unpublished paper read at the Spring Meeting of the Association of Social Anthropologists, 1961, 'Economic Preconditions of Social Stratification', M. Douglas.

4

Industrial Britain

Institutionalized social inequality can be seen fairly clearly in those societies where the rectitude and excellence of different characters and actions are (or were) expressed in law and religious doctrine. It was plainly stated in Hindu doctrine that Brahmans were superior; and the legal code of feudal Japan was unambiguous on the deference due to samurai and sanctioned the imposition of physical, economic and psychological punishments for 'other than expected' behaviour. But in Britain today the prevailing social value is the equality of men, not envisaging the sameness of men but the provision of equal opportunity for advancement with the onus placed upon the individual for his own social standing. No longer can fate or accident of birth or the wicked aristocracy be invoked as a legitimate reason for social failure. The fault is said to reside in the individual for not trying hard enough.

Is social stratification, therefore, non-existent? Are there no rank orders with varying degrees of prestige attached? Are there no social attitudes and activities which are inimical to the full realization of the value of equal opportunity? Answers are still being sought but enough evidence is available to show that Britain is a stratified society and that there are social attitudes and activities which impede the implementation of the value of equal opportunity, for they diminish and prevent equal access to opportunities.

Social grading of occupations

One characteristic of individuals which has been found to be evaluated is occupation. Hall and Jones (1950) prepared a list of thirty occupations, then asked 1,400 people to arrange them in descending order of prestige. The result was 'a large measure of agreement' on the following order of occupational groups:

1. Professional and high administrative; occupations which call for highly specialized experience and frequently a university degree or comparable professional qualification,
2. Managerial and executive; those responsible for initiating and/or implementing policy,
3. Inspectional, supervisory and other non-manual, higher grade; no such responsibility as associated with managerial and executive but with some degree of authority over others,
4. Inspectional, supervisory and other non-manual, lower grade,
5. Skilled manual and routine grades of non-manual,
6. Semi-skilled manual and
7. Unskilled manual.

Some of the disagreement noted was associated with the occupational grade of the individual doing the ranking, those in higher grades tending to show more consistency than those in lower grades in placing specific occupations in the prestige levels (Moser and Hall, in Glass, 1954), perhaps because of a slight inclination to downgrade those occupations of putatively higher prestige than their own, perhaps because of differing ideas of who ought to receive high esteem through his occupational activities. As graders in lower occupational ranks made up a very small proportion of the total graders, these inclinations could not be explored to any great extent.

A later study by Young and Willmott (1956) has helped to clarify the situation somewhat. They asked eighty-two respondents, nearly half of whom were manual workers, to rate the same thirty occupations. The ratings made by these respondents varied, from those consistent with the Hall and Jones' study to those where the order was very nearly totally reversed. The rankings of sixty respondents were fairly similar to the previous study but twenty-two respondents showed considerable deviance. In an attempt to understand this phenomenon Young and Willmott asked the raters why they judged the occupations as they did and how they would rate their own jobs. The rating criteria fell into five categories: ability, education, remuneration, social milieu and social contribution. While the group which showed consistency with the Hall and Jones' findings were using intelligence, skill and education to rate the occupations, the 'deviants' were using social contribution with the result that agricultural labourers, coal miners and bricklayers were highly rated because 'They're absolutely essential' while clerks, accountants, business managers and company directors were placed well down the list—'They get their money for just standing around'. The 'deviant' raters, with one exception, were manual workers, thus indicating a possible lack of consensus over who should and who should not be accorded high esteem.

A study like this needs to be repeated many times to

clarify the issue but it is sufficient as a warning to those who appear convinced that there is a consensus over which positions are considered more highly than others. With this caution in mind, occupation will be used to see if the distribution of rewards and access to opportunities are consistent with an occupational gradient.

Physical life chances

The analysis of morbidity and mortality statistics by the General Registry Office has shown that occupation is associated with different chances of living and dying and sickness and health. Broad occupational groups are used, first arranged in a rough, *ad hoc* order of rank explained in a paper to the Royal Statistical Society in 1928 by Dr. T. H. C. Stevenson. That mortality rates could be explained solely on the basis of wealth and poverty was not convincing to Stevenson; he believed that culture, intelligence and education could exert powerful influences, illustrating his argument by the case of clergymen, often poor but frequently long-lived. He thought that social position could be inferred through broad occupational groups as they were indicative of differential opportunities and cultural milieux in a society. Accordingly, five groups had been proposed: (1) upper and middle classes, (2) intermediate between 1 and 3, (3) skilled workmen, (4) intermediate between 3 and 5 and (5) unskilled workmen. Stevenson considered the scheme successful as he had found from the 1921 Census that natality and mortality varied regularly though not uniformly with the different occupational levels. In general, this classification is still used, only some of the names have changed as have the number and kind of occupations in each category and it is assumed that the occupations within each category are homogeneous with respect to social standing in the community. To avoid tedious repetition the categories below will be referred to as R.G.I., R.G.II, R.G.III, R.G.IV and R.G.V.:

Social Class I   Professional and similar occupations,
Social Class II   Intermediate (I and III) occupations,
Social Class III Skilled occupations,
Social Class IV   Partly skilled occupations and
Social Class V   Unskilled occupations.

Particular occupations included in these categories can be found listed in the Registrar General's *Classification of Occupations* and discussion concerning the placement of occupations into social classes can be found in the introductory notes to the *Occupational Mortality Tables*.

Infant mortality

Infant mortality rates show an occupational gradient even though incomes and health standards have risen in this country during the century.

TABLE 1

Mortality rates for infants under one year per 1000 live births
1949–1950

Occupational Group	Mortality Rate
R.G.I	16·9
R.G.II	19·9
R.G.III	26·2
R.G.IV	31·7
R.G.V	36·0

(Heady and Heasman 1959)

Consultations with doctors

Without systematic and continuous surveys of the general population, morbidity rates or a measure of the prevalence of particular diseases and illnesses cannot be validly established. However, inroads on this problem were made by Dr. Logan (1960) of the General Registry Office in a study of seventy-six general practices representing about one hundred and twenty practitioners from May 1955 to April 1956, using a patient consulting ratio as a measure of morbidity, i.e., the number of patients, standardized by sex, age and occupational group, who consulted their doctors at least once during the survey period. The classification of occupations into non-manual and manual by patient consulting ratios showed that the 'morbidity' of psycho-neurotic and cardio-vascular disorders was high amongst non-manual workers, while that of respiratory and gastric disorders, arthritis and rheumatism and injuries was high amongst manual workers.

Mortality

During the period 1949 to 1953, males classified as R.G.IV and R.G.V. were more likely to die between the ages of twenty and sixty-four than were males classified R.G.I, II or III (Registrar General, 1958). Causes of death also tended to differ according to occupational categories with higher social categories more often associated with acute poliomyelitis, leukaemia, coronary disease and angina and hypertension; and lower social categories more often associated with tuberculosis, malignant neoplasms, chronic rheumatic heart disease, influenza, pneumonia and bronchitis—to name a few (Registrar General, 1958).

Differences are not confined to physical diseases, for American work has shown that in the case of mental health, those of a higher social standing are more likely to be admitted to psychiatric clinics and receive a longer treatment of a higher quality than accrue to those in lower ranks (Myers and Schaffer, 1954), although other work indicates that mental ill health is more prevalent in the lower ranks (Hollingshead and Redlich, 1958).

Many differential advantages are associated with broad occupational groups and associated in such a way that followers of those occupations which were said to carry higher prestige than others tend to be positively privileged in their physical life chances: their children are less likely to die in infancy; they appear less susceptible to many physical diseases; they are less likely to die between the ages of twenty and sixty-four; and when they become mentally ill, they are more likely to be treated by more highly qualified practitioners for a longer period of time.

Socio-economic life chances

The advantages already noted accrue to a relatively small proportion of the population. Occupations classified as Social Classes I and II by the Registrar General in 1951 constituted about 19% of the occupied and retired adult population, 3% in R.G.I. and 16% in R.G.II, the rest of the population being divided into R.G.III, IV and V with respective percentages of 52, 17 and 12. By the exclusion of agricultural workers and members of the armed forces, a classification by non-manual and manual occupations gives a percentage division of 35 and 65. To the few go the prizes.

Occupation

A more detailed division of the nearly thirty million people in the occupied and retired adult population in 1951 (this includes males; single, widowed and divorced women and married women enumerated with their husbands) was made by the General Registry Office by the assignment of occupations to socio-economic groups. Although the Hall-Jones scale and the Registrar General's

TABLE 2

Proportions of the population classified into the Registrar General's socio-economic groups arranged in rough order of decreasing prestige as judged from the Hall-Jones Scale
(in per cent)

R.G.'s Socio-Economic Groups	Hall-Jones Occupational Groups	Proportion of the Population %
Higher administrative, professional and managerial	Professional managerial and executive	3·0
Other administrative, professional and managerial	Inspectional, supervisory and other non-manual higher grade	10·4
Shopkeepers and foremen	Other inspectional, supervisory and non-manual, lower grade	7·1
Clerical workers, shop assistants and skilled manual workers	Skilled manual and routine non-manual workers	44·8
Personal service and semi-skilled manual workers	Semi-skilled manual workers	15·5
Unskilled manual workers	Unskilled manual workers	11·3

(Percentages do not add up to one hundred because farmers, agricultural workers and armed forces, other ranks, have been excluded.)

49

socio-economic classifications are not strictly comparable, some indication of the proportions of the population receiving differential advantages can be gained by arranging the socio-economic groups in a roughly similar order to that of the Hall-Jones scale.

Income

In a recent nationwide survey conducted by the Ministry of Labour (1963) on family expenditure, distributions of the total income per household and the income of heads of households in relation to the occupation of the head of the household were noted. When the income of only the head of the household was considered, 78% of non-manual households earned £15 or more per week as opposed to about 52% of manual households. This gap between non-manual and manual incomes is somewhat reduced when the total income of each household is considered because of the greater number of wage earners per household in the manual group.[1]

Residence

Those people with occupations which carry similar social prestige tend to live in the same areas of a city, so that frequently, the social honour of a family may be deduced from their address (Warner, 1960). An excellent account of differences in types of housing, furnishing and their usages in the Liverpool area (1950) as these are related to social prestige can be found in *The Home and Social Status* by Dennis Chapman, so that only three differences will be considered here; population density, the proportion of households in shared dwellings and the number of persons per room; the last two factors

[1] I am indebted to Elizabeth Gittus for these tabulations.

being frequently referred to as 'overcrowding'. In the Merseyside area, those sections which had the largest proportions of households classified as R.G.I and II also had the lowest population density, the lowest proportion of households in shared dwellings, and the lowest number of persons per room (data for 1951) (Gittus, 1960). The physical comforts associated with high social prestige are difficult to ignore.

Education

A survey of the educational experience of the adult population up to July 1949 has revealed further evidence of an occupational gradient in relation to the distribution of life chances (Floud, in Glass, 1954). Attendance at elementary and independent schools was noted according to the status category (Hall and Jones) of the students' fathers and it was seen that substantially larger proportions of children of professional, managerial and executive fathers attended independent schools than did those with fathers in lower status categories.

TABLE 3

Primary schooling in relation to the status category of the father in per cent of each status category

Primary School Attended	Status Category of Father						Total
	1	2	3	4	5	6 & 7	
Elementary	44·9	69·3	84·9	91·9	97·1	98·9	92·8
Independent	55·1	30·7	15·1	8·1	2·9	1·1	7·2
Total	100%	100%	100%	100%	100%	100%	100%

(Floud, in Glass, 1954)

Although children of fathers in status categories 1 and 2

made up only 7·2% of the total attending both kinds of schools, they accounted for 42% of the total attending independent schools.[2]

Further significance of these different educational chances is evident in progression to secondary education; for of those who attended elementary school, 9·7% went on to secondary grammar or boarding schools whereas 72·3% of those who attended independent primary schools did so (Floud in Glass, 1954).

This differential selection continues in further education as was seen in the *Report of the Central Advisory Council for Education, England, 1960*. Of school leavers (boys) in 1954 and 1955, about 10% were engaged in full-time education, 6% of these being grammar and

[2]Table 4. Attendance at Primary Schools in relation to the status category of the father in per cent of the total number of pupils, Hall-Jones status categories.

Status Categories	% of the Survey Population in Each Status Category Attending Both Kinds of Primary School	% of the Survey Population in Each Status Category Attending Independent Schools
1	3·2	24·8
2	4·0	17·2
3	9·8	20·6
4	14·4	16·2
5	43·6	17·6
6 & 7	24·8	3·7
Total	99·8%	100·1%
N equals	7873	569

(Source: Floud, in Glass, 1954)

technical school boys, the rest, modern and all-age school boys. For these two groups the type of further education differed, university education being associated with the first group along with professional and managerial fathers. A more recent survey has shown that

> ... children with fathers in professional and managerial occupations are twenty times more likely to enter full-time education than are those with fathers in semi- and unskilled jobs. (*Higher Education, 1963*).

That this differential was not totally dependent upon intelligence as measured by I.Q. tests is seen from Table 5. In every case, with similar I.Q. scores at 11 plus, higher proportions of children whose fathers had non-manual occupations entered a degree-level course of higher education.

Table 5

Highest course of education entered by children from Maintained Grammar Schools and Senior Secondary Schools in Scotland: in relation to I.Q. at 11 Plus and fathers' occupation, Great Britain, children born in 1941 in Per Cent

NM: non-manual, M: manual

I.Q.	Higher Education		Other	Total
	Full-Time	*Part-Time*		
	Degree Level	*Other*		
130 plus				
NM	37	4	10	48	100%
M	18	12	10	60	100%
115–129				
NM	17	17	4	61	100%
M	8	7	9	76	100%
100–114				
NM	6	11	8	75	100%
M	2	4	7	87	100%

(*Higher Education*, 1963)

Summary

There is evidence, then, of a distribution of physical and socio-economic life chances along occupational lines; and, further, that the occupational gradients of these distributions correspond somewhat with that seen in the social grading of occupations. Those occupations which were placed on higher social levels than others tended to be the same as those whose followers were positively advantaged in the acquisition of life's prizes. The value that one 'gets on' because of ability would appear to be realized by the association of educational attainment with occupations of high prestige but there also appear to be social factors which influence this individual ability. Factors other than intelligence as measured in I.Q. tests seem operative in restricting and facilitating access to occupations judged desirable by many people.

Before we consider some of these, it would be as well to note that many of the problems concerning the distribution and measurement of prestige are still with us. If ability and intelligence are highly valued, does this mean that ability in all directions brings prestige or that only certain kinds of ability are desirable? If the latter, what are these kinds of ability? Do different kinds of ability attract different kinds of prestige? Indeed, is prestige accorded in terms of continuous increments or does it come in discrete blocks? Where does one prestige level stop and another begin? Are there systems of prestige levels in our society other than that based upon occupation? If so, are the various systems interconnected? Even in the case of the ranking of occupations, recent American work complements the Young and Willmott study in suggesting that not all those who grade occupations to produce an occupational rank order are making their judgments according to the same criteria (Gusfield and Schwartz, 1963). Some are judging according to the assumed money return attached to the occupation; some are judging occupations as they think others would judge them; while others are rating occupations as they think they ought to be rated, not as they think they are rated; and still others are considering occupations as honourable and dishonourable to follow regardless of the remuneration attached.

With these qualifications in mind, we will consider some of the attitudes and activities which have been found to be associated with followers of different occupations.

5

Life styles and occupations

Family and kin

That lower income families tend to be larger than higher income families is a finding that has become so much a part of popular knowledge that the 'tendency' indicated in the finding has been transformed into a certainty, thereby obscuring the complexities which underlie it. In an analysis of data from the 1951 Census, Dennis Wrong (1960) has pointed out a continuing differential in family size, in that for all ages at marriage and for all durations of marriage, the number of live born children for each one hundred once-married women showed an increasing gradient from the Registrar General's Social Class I to Social Class V—R.G.I: 141; R.G.II: 149; R.G.III: 165; R.G.IV: 196 and R.G.V: 217. Marsh (1958) has noted, however, that marked differences in family size have been diminishing over the years so that the only one which still remains is the slightly greater prevalence of three or more children in households where the occupation of the head of the household places it in R.G. Social Classes IV and V.

Although the gap in the size of families classified as non-manual and manual has been closing, largely due to the decrease in the number of children in households whose head is a manual worker, for those who have been married for five years or less (the assumption here being that their families have not yet been completed), this non-manual/manual split appears to be widening (see D. H. Wrong, 1960). This may mean either that manual workers marry younger and complete their families sooner, in which case the difference in family size between non-manual and manual workers will not increase, or they marry younger and have more children, in which case the differences will increase. In a sample of eighteen-year olds and over in England and Wales in 1949 a significant difference in the average age at marriage was found between non-manual and manual workers, the latter group marrying earlier (Mukherjee in Glass, 1954). From the Newsons' study of infant care in Nottingham (1963) has come evidence that the average age of mothers at the birth of their first child tended to be lower where the father's occupation was classified as R.G.V. rather than R.G.I. II or III non-manual. The Newsons also found that there was a higher percentage of families with three or more children in manual groups than in non-manual groups. There is evidence that more non-manual families practice birth control than manual families; for of those married during the years 1950 to 1960 the relevant percentages were 79 and 66 (Pierce, 1961). If these trends were to continue, we would expect to find that the difference in the size of non-manual and manual families would persist.

However, a factor which could influence this trend is movement across occupational lines, for Douglas and Blomfield (1958) have found that those families who were moving up the social scale had fewer children than the average for the group from whence they came while those moving down the social scale had more.

The significance of family size in relation to social opportunities tends to be evident principally in the case of children of manual workers and those in borderline non-manual/manual occupations; for Halsey and Gardner (1953) have found that

> Working class boys who do attend these schools [Grammar Schools] are more likely to be from small families than large families, and whatever the size of their families, tend to be eldest children rather than of later birth order and neither of these conditions applies to the middle-class boy.

Perhaps the two best known works on social class differences and child rearing are the Newsons' study in Nottingham and the work done in the United States by Sears, Maccoby and Levin (*Patterns of Child Rearing*, 1957). The Newsons have noted that there are broad similarities in child rearing within class lines. Their data show that in general, working class mothers are more indulgent in allowing the extensive use of bottles and dummies and in later bedtimes, are less likely to succeed in the toilet training of children up to one year of age and are more punitive as indicated by a greater use of smacking for one-year olds and less permissiveness of genital play.

Josephine Klein's (1965) summary of the American work shows the same trends of working class indulgence and punitiveness and middle class permissiveness and tolerance.

> It was found that all the better-educated mothers, regardless of their social position, and all middle-class mothers, regardless of their educational level, were

likely to be less severe in their toilet training, more permissive about childish evidence of sexual impulses, more permissive about childish aggression toward themselves, less likely to punish their children corporally or by depriving them of privileges, and more ambitious for them at school than their less educated or more working-class sisters. Middle-class mothers, whether their schooling had been prolonged or not, were more likely to be affectionate and demonstrative to their children and less likely to display signs of rejection; they tended not to use ridicule as a technique of controlling the child (which might have impaired the children's self-esteem) and used isolation more (which encourages the child to think and to depend more on his own resources).

... Bronfenbrenner sums up the mothers at the more privileged end of the social scale as being more tolerant of the child's expressed needs and less punitive in their approach, but also as expecting more from the child in the way of self-control and willingness to please or make an effort.

The kind of relationships which exist between members of a family are of crucial importance in circumscribing the life experiences of children. One such relationship is that between husband and wife and has to do with the degree of segregation in their activities both inside and outside of the home, referred to as conjugal role segregation (see E. Bott, *Family and Social Network*, 1957). A high degree of conjugal role segregation involves a strict division of labour between husband and wife so that tasks hardly ever overlap. The husband brings home the money, decides how much to give to his wife as her 'wages' and keeps the rest for himself, the wife not knowing the husband's total income. With the fixed sum given

59

to her the wife has to provide for the husband's comfort and rear the children because they are her responsibility. The husband offers no assistance in household tasks and the wife never asks for such assistance. The wife expects her husband to have his own friends with whom he spends much of his leisure time at football matches and in clubs and pubs, while what leisure time the wife has is spent in visiting with and helping her kinfolk. Husband and wife seldom share leisure activities and infrequently entertain 'friends', defined as non-kinfolk, in the home. The cartoon character 'Andy Capp' presents a rather exaggerated portrait of this kind of life. A less strict division of labour between husband and wife means that there is more consultation between them as to how the money should be spent, how the children should be brought up and what kind of leisure activities should be encouraged. Tasks in the home are shared, the husband helping his wife with cooking, washing up, repairing, gardening and looking after children.

Dr. Bott has suggested that the degree of segregation of activities of husband and wife depends upon how connected their social relationships are outside the immediate family, that is, of those people whom a husband and wife know, the number who in turn know each other. A 'close-knit' network means that many of the people whom one knows also know each other while a 'loose-knit' network means that few of the people whom one knows also know each other. Those husbands and wives with close-knit networks are more likely to exhibit a high degree of conjugal role segregation than are those with more loose-knit networks; and close-knit networks and a high degree of conjugal role segregation tend to be more characteristic of manual rather than non-manual workers, particularly of manual workers who have lived in one part of a city all their lives, the same part in which their fathers and grandfathers had lived. These factors of geographical immobility, everyone knowing everyone else and a strict division of labour for the sexes help to identify a particular way of life which is referred to as 'traditional' because it has been accepted as given by those involved, allows few opportunities for choice and prescribes punitive sanctions for deviants.

Young and Willmott (1957) found that in Bethnal Green some families considered that a grammar school education for a working class child was not right. There was definite pressure exerted against such an education both by friends and parents, the former made fun of the uniform while the latter were convinced that the mixture of education and working people was immoral. Because everyone knew everyone else a united front could be shown to an individual who wished to experiment, who wished to be different, so that such an individual would have to face the psychological consequences of social isolation or leave the area if he persisted in his experimentation.

A traditional way of life is not confined to manual workers, however; it can be found at all social levels. Those who are enmeshed in such a life are convinced of its moral rectitude and just as convinced of the moral iniquity of those with different views and different ways of behaving. For example, Margaret Stacey (1960) was confronted with an aspect of traditional middle class life through the advice given to a newcomer by a Colonel's wife:

'I think you'll like the X's,' she said, 'and there are the Y's and the Z's; otherwise I don't think there is anybody. But of course it's bad luck for you there are no children in the village.' (The newcomer had a young family.) Happily this startling picture of rural depopulation was contradicted by statistics which showed that the village had a population of about five hundred with a normal complement of children. Yet this woman ... referred to 98% of her fellow-villagers as 'nobody' ...

Although traditional ways of life are found at all social levels, that found amongst manual workers seems most likely to restrict horizons, reduce the scope of experimentation and limit the chances for new experiences. If these restrictions occurred in societies where no great stress was placed on achievement and success, individualism and the rational adjustment of means to ends, they would not be felt as restrictions—but we are concerned with twentieth-century Britain. To attain a greater security of employment and a higher standard of living and to realize the values of achievement, individualism and rationality, a manual worker must climb the educational ladder; yet his traditional way of life works against this through the way he is socialized and the close-knit network which protects him but also acts as a barrier to change.

The combination of indulgence and punitiveness in the socialization process in working class families has been said to encourage an arbitrary socialization in which the child learns to obey the person in authority because he or she is in authority rather than because a principle of life is being exemplified. Obedience is demanded on a personal rather than an impersonal basis; as, for example, in the contrast between 'You be good because I said so' and 'You be good because if you are too difficult to get on with, you will have no friends when you grow up'. This kind of socialization is said to make it difficult to generalize one's experiences, to construct principles of action within which variation is allowed and is likely to produce anxiety when the person enters a new situation until he learns 'what he is supposed to do.'

This anxiety is exacerbated by the factor of 'cognitive poverty', the lack of generalizing words in one's vocabulary. Following Luria (1959, 1960), Basil Bernstein (1958, 1959) has produced evidence for the existence of two speech codes, (restricted and elaborated) which involve not only words but also the way the words are organized. A public language results from a restricted form of organizing speech and tends to limit one's perception to the obvious, personal and concrete in the environment; or at least limit one's ability to communicate anything but the immediately obvious, personal and concrete. Communication via a public language is successful only when all involved in the communication are part of the same tradition, so much a part that shades of meaning and feeling are communicated non-verbally by gestures and voice inflections standardized over the years. Through the use of a formal language, however, different meanings and feelings can be conveyed through the arrangement of words and connections between sentences. This code is used by both middle class and working class children but Bernstein's evidence seems to indicate that lower working class children have access only to a public language while others have access to both a public and a formal language (the result of an elaborated speech code).

Whereas a public language tends to limit curiosity by the use of a relatively few traditional, idiomatic phrases, a formal language is a more adequate vehicle for exploration and experimentation. In a public language the legitimacy for the statement made resides in the form of the social relationship which is non-verbally present ('Do that because I told you to.') rather than in its logic or rationality. In Bernstein's view the implications of the sole use of a public language are far-reaching: the encouragement of a preference for a particular form of social relationship, one where individual qualifications are non-verbally communicated, a relationship which is inclusive rather than demanding the involvement of only a small part of the personality; the inculcation of sensitivity to demands of solidarity and a socially induced conservatism, a resistance to certain forms of change which would alter the organization of the local group; encouragement to accept and respond to the authority pattern exhibited by the communicator and receiver rather than to a reasoned or logical principle and emphasis on loyalty to the goals of a local group more than to more complex aims found in the major society.

Josephine Klein derived many of these implications from data on community studies which she reviewed and related them to cognitive poverty; for example, (1) the presence in many working class areas of large families and relatively low standards of living with less contact observed between working class mothers and their children, (2) children learning from and conversing with other children more than from and with adults, (3) the indulgence of the working class mother which was unpredictable to the child so that he had to guess from her emotional state whether or not he would be punished for a particular act, (4) her punitiveness when she decided not to be indulgent, (5) the general unpredictability of mother-child relationships until the child could respond not to *what* was said but *how* it was said, (6) the resultant difficulty of the child in handling general concepts and principles because of lack of teaching and (7) the inability to plan for future behaviour because of the lack of predictability in the responses of the mother. Predictability, long-term planning, the postponement of immediate gain for the sake of future rewards, all characteristic of the middle classes and associated with success in formal schooling; these were foreign to a child in a traditional working class situation. The traditional middle class milieu, however, although restricted and resistant to change, was nevertheless developmental in nature as the socialization process encouraged verbalization and individual thought.

Leisure activities

Much evidence has been produced to show that manual workers are not 'joiners', and of those manual workers who do join organizations and associations few aspire to and/or achieve positions of leadership. In the Cauter and Downham (1954) study of Derby it was found that 58% of the working class belonged to no clubs or associations as opposed to 42% of the middle class; however, this difference was not consistently demonstrated when the working class group was further divided into skilled and semi- and unskilled workers. On the basis of their data it can be said that skilled manual workers can be characterized as joiners in the same degree as non-manual workers can be, for there is no significant difference between manual and non-manual workers in respect of the proportions of each who belonged to no club or association.

The Cauter and Downham data show differences in patterns of associations in the two large occupational categories, not that non-manual workers are joiners and manual workers are non-joiners. For example 68% of the manual workers were members of trade unions and professional bodies while the corresponding figure for non-manual workers was 43%. A higher percentage of manual than non-manual workers joined social clubs and sports' associations while the position was reversed with respect to cultural organizations. Manual workers join clubs and associations as much as non-manual workers, and in some cases more so, but they join different kinds of clubs. They seem to join the less formal association, the one which requires less conscious efforts at sociability because the members are friends, neighbours, workmates. The less formal association by definition has a relatively flexible authority structure and is not involved in long-term planning. Each member of the association plays approximately the same part in the activities so that no one member is indispensable in keeping the club going. A member does not feel compelled to attend every meeting but can drift in and out as the spirit moves; and as the membership is drawn from a relatively small geographical area, members are more likely to know each other from different contexts (the close-knit network) and less likely to be of different social classes, so that the effort required to communicate across class barriers is eliminated (Klein, 1965).

In those associations where the membership cuts across class boundaries, leadership positions tend to fall to non-manual workers. In a study of stratification in voluntary organizations Thomas Bottomore (Glass, 1954) found that higher occupational groups contributed more than their share to leadership positions as judged from their percentage of the membership; Group A being members with professional, technical, managerial and executive occupations, Group B, members with other non-manual, salaried occupations and Group C, members with manual and routine non-manual weekly-paid occupations.

The difference is greatest for Group A which provides 16·6% of the members, but 62% of the officials, and for Group C which provides 60·4% of the members but only 18·2% of the officials. In the case of Group B there is more symmetry, with 23% of the members and 19·8% of the officials coming from this group.

In many organizations positions of leadership and followership tend to mirror those in the larger society.

Ideas and values

Differences in hopes and plans for the future and ideas about children and life in general have been implied in much of the preceding material, so that only a few will be discussed here. In 1950 F. M. Martin (Glass, 1954) found significant differences with regard to aspirations for children amongst adults: 76% of those classified as professional middle class wanted their children to stay at school until at least eighteen years of age whereas only 29% of those classified as manual working class wished this for their children.

Attitudes towards education varied amongst children as well as adults. Of 317 boys in their third year of secondary education, two-thirds of the middle and working class boys having I.Q.'s of over 115, 62% of the middle class boys said that they would like to stay in school after they were sixteen if they were free to do as they wished, whereas only 45% of the working class boys expressed such a desire (Bene, 1959). Many studies have shown that concern with how well children do at school, higher educational aspirations, long-term vocational plans, more supervision of schoolwork and play and a more rigid system of values tend to be more characteristic of middle class than working class families (Floud, Halsey and Anderson, 1961). In middle class families there is more encouragement for the display of imagination and the setting up of long-term goals toward which the child works slowly but surely. The inculcation of such attitudes is a great aid in adjusting to the atmosphere of the school, and as will be seen in the next section, nearly indispensable for occupational and social mobility.

Recent work has emphasized that those in different social positions in a society also hold different views of the nature of that society (Goldthorpe and Lockwood, 1963); that

> ...among groups of individuals occupying comparable positions within the social hierarchy, a broadly similar 'social imagery' tended to occur...

Amongst manual workers the stratification system is described as dichotomous (Them and Us), while non-manual workers tend to describe the stratification system in terms of levels or strata arranged in a hierarchy of differentially rewarded positions. They see both the possibility and the desirability of moving from one prestige level to another through individual effort; but for the manual workers the split between Them and Us is practically insurmountable. Implied in these responses are two different kinds of society; one composed of levels of positions separated by a formidable chasm transversed only by group effort, the other composed of several levels, between which movement is possible through individual effort, with great emphasis being placed upon the efficacy of such effort rather than upon group action. The simplified version of the stratification system attributed more to manual than non-manual workers appears to tie in with many characteristics noted before which are associated with the close-knit network, traditional working class life and cognitive poverty. An important question now is, how does geographical mobility and education affect these images? When manual workers migrate from settled neighbourhoods and reduce the intensity and frequency of contacts with their close-knit kin networks, do they and/or their children come to accept middle class values and middle class images of the society?

Mobility

Although geographical mobility is not unknown to manual workers (Royal Commission, 1940), it is only with the fairly recent programmes of slum clearance and the establishment of new towns that many working class families have pulled up their roots and restructured life in new surroundings. For example, in 1944 three-quarters of the heads of families in Bethnal Green were born in the borough (Robb, 1954). In 1949 a Government Social Survey on occupational and job mobility showed that 87% of all occupational and industrial changes took place within the local community while only 13% of the changes resulted in movement between towns in different regions (Thomas, 1953). Of the manual workers the skilled are most likely to change their residence and apart from the extreme case of a small group of people in scientific, technical and administrative careers (called 'spiralists' because of their frequent changes of residence in the cause of furthering their careers (Susser and Watson, 1962)), skilled workers contribute considerably to the entire mobile population.

Social stability and social mobility are two sides of the coin of social placement because the two methods of recruitment to occupational positions are by direct inheritance of a position by the son and by movement into the position either from above or below. If this movement occurs within an individual's life span, it is referred to as 'intragenerational mobility', if it occurs within two or more generations, the term applied is 'intergenerational mobility'. Many factors influence the

F

chances of social mobility, some of the more important being the kind of economy in a society, birth rates and death rates in occupational levels. For example, in a complex, industrial society where the level of technology allows movement towards more automation, one would expect an increase in technical and supervisory jobs rather than unskilled or routine clerical work, as machines are developed to take over heavy and repetitive work. Other things being equal, one would also expect an increase in service occupations if more leisure time were available to greater numbers as a result of mechanical aids. However, there is always the possibility that members of some occupational groups could and would choose not to increase the number of jobs within their spheres in hopes of maintaining or increasing the value of their labour by restricting access to training. Birth and death rates in high status groups also are major factors in determining the availability of high status positions, and in industrialized (but not in all industrializing) societies the general rule is for the birth rate to go down as income and status positions go up. On the basis of considerable comparative evidence, Lipset and Bendix (1959) have concluded that complex industrial societies offer more chances for upward social mobility than those with less technical development.

Data collected in the late 1940's (Lipset and Bendix, 1959) show similarities in intragenerational mobility for non-manual and manual workers taken as broad groups but important variations amongst subdivisions of these groups: the professions were the most static with 80% of professionals having begun and remained at that level; those beginning as clerks were about equally likely to stay as clerks or move up or down the social scale. Of the manual groups about half of those who started in skilled work stayed in such work, the same being true of semi-skilled workers; the least stable group was unskilled workers of whom only 26% who started in unskilled work, stayed in unskilled work. The manual/ non-manual line was more of a barrier for the semi- and unskilled worker than for the skilled, as only 2% of the former group moved to clerking positions while 38% of the latter moved one level or more as far as the managerial stratum (this included supervisory positions) (Thomas, 1953).

The measurement of mobility between generations is a very difficult task (Smelser & Lipset, 1966) so that, frequently, one infers intergenerational mobility from changes over time in the composition of occupational levels, composition being defined as occupations of fathers of sons in various occupations. It is seen from the same Lipset and Bendix data that the proportion of sons of fathers with non-manual occupations who moved to manual work (49%) was higher than that of sons of fathers in manual occupations who moved to non-manual work (20%); these figures not being too different from those in the United States, contrary to popular myths. This finding has yet to be reconciled with many others which point to the conclusion that sons of non-manual fathers have greater chances of upward mobility and fewer chances of downward mobility than do sons of manual fathers.

As in the case of mobility within one's lifetime, chances for intergenerational changes in occupational status differ for occupational groups. Glass and Hall (Glass, 1954) found that skilled manual and routine non-manual workers had the highest relative mobility of all the status groups, while there was considerable self-recruitment in professional, high administrative, managerial and executive occupational groups. The inspectional and supervisory and semi- and unskilled manual groups showed more self-recruitment than the skilled manual and routine non-manual groups but less than the higher status groups. A separate study of sons following in fathers' footsteps in four professions; teaching, medicine, the church and law, showed that high proportions of students whose fathers were in one of the four professions mentioned above had been trained or were in the process of being trained for one of these professions (Kelsall in Glass, 1954). The correspondence noted earlier between professional status of the father and university education of the son should take much of the surprise away from the finding of considerable self-recruitment in the professions.

With some notable exceptions, members of the business elite are sons of fathers whose occupations placed them in higher status groups. Of 1,243 directors in British industry questioned by Copemen (1955), 51% were sons of businessmen, 22%, sons of professional and administrative workers and only 8% originated from the lower middle and working classes. Clements (1958) has noted that those with higher social origins experienced more rapid promotion, a higher average salary and a good chance of getting on the board. Graduate engineers who were being interviewed for management positions were more likely to have come from top social status groups than those lower down the scale.

As occupation appears to be a major guide to a person's social status in our society and only a minority of women have full time, paid occupations, to a considerable degree a woman's social status is reflected from that of her husband's and/or father's. Her first opportunity, and frequently her only opportunity, for social mobility occurs at marriage. If the value of improving oneself is held with the intensity that one suspects, it is not remarkable that women tend to marry 'above themselves' more often than do men (Berent, in Glass, 1954); not that this is the only reason for the phenomenon, but women appear to have more at stake when marriage vows are uttered. The stability found in the professional and high administrative, managerial and executive groups with respect to self-recruitment to occupational positions occurs again in the selection of mates. Men in these status groups are very likely to marry women who are daughters of other men in these status groups. This endogamy is more intense than in any of the other status groups. The least intense endogamy is found amongst skilled manual and routine non-manual workers. However, the social origins of brides and grooms seem less important than their own education, for of all the cases Berent (Glass, 1954) analysed, 45% occurred between mates of similar social origins whereas over 71% occurred between partners of similar educational level with '... the least marital mobility ... among individuals who have had university or other higher education'.

Summary

We have seen that there are differences between classes and differences between status groups within classes. Amongst manual workers there is a traditional group in which one notes larger families, close-knit kin networks and highly segregated husband-wife relationships, indulgence-punitiveness patterns in raising children, cognitive poverty, relatively narrow social and cultural horizons, little geographical mobility and circumscribed social mobility. The non-traditional group shows more of an individualistic than a collectivistic outlook and in many respects shows a life style similar to that of the middle classes. Within the middle classes the higher status groups keep themselves more to themselves in the way of marriage and recruitment to higher status occupations. The delineation of status groups within classes is by no means complete so that it is very likely that further research will show that the actual situation is very much more complicated than we have presented it at the moment. Studies of communities have shown more complex pictures of social stratification than nationwide investigations. For example, in one Welsh community social prestige seems to be based upon religious affiliation (Jenkins, Jones, Hughes and Owen, 1960) and its consequent life style while other community studies (Warner and Lunt, 1942) show length of residence and family background to be very important in the allocation of social honour. The challenge to understand the structure and workings of social stratification both in general and in specific societies sharpens with each addition to knowledge.

6

Changes in social stratification in Britain

Without adequate measures of the rates of change in the various aspects of social stratification, the speed of change, or the lack of it, depends upon one's own viewpoint. For those who long for 'the good old days when everyone knew his place', such changes as have been discerned have been decried as coming too suddenly to produce anything but degeneration and chaos. To those who hope for a 'new society', even a snail goes faster.

Changes at the top

The men who reach the pinnacles of political, business and civil service careers do not have the same social origins as did their predecessors in the late nineteenth- and early twentieth-centuries. The proportion of cabinet ministers from non-manual backgrounds dropped from 96% during the period 1886 to 1916 to 72% in the 1916 to 1955 span, the proportion with manual backgrounds rising from 3 to 16% (Guttsman, 1963). Eighty per cent of the political elite from 1868 to 1886 consisted of aristocrats by descent, landowners or men educated at Eton, Harrow, Winchester, Rugby, Shrewsbury, Charterhouse and Westminster, but from 1935 to 1955 this proportion dropped to just about half of the political notables. The upper professional, the barrister and lawyer, the academic (Vice-Chancellors and the heads of Oxbridge colleges), the retired civil servant and military chief, these rather than aristocrats and landowners are appearing in the ranks of the political elites, these who are referred to as the upper middle class (Guttsman, 1963).

There exists today in Britain a 'ruling class', if we mean by it a group which provides the majority of those who occupy positions of power, and who, in their turn, can materially assist *their* sons to reach similar positions.

The name is the same but the personnel has changed.

In his study of managers in twenty-eight firms in the Manchester area, Clements (1958) found that these firms still tended to recruit their managers and technicians from upper social strata, despite fluctuations in emphasis on the type of manager appointed. Vacancies created by the war offered only temporary increases in chances for the promotion of those in lower social groups. It may be expected that a higher proportion of future managers will be recruited from the lower middle and middle classes if the demand for the 'trained expert' continues, for Clements noted that many such experts had degrees from provincial universities and included many men with these middle class origins. The proportion of men with working class origins is likely to decrease unless more use can be made by them of the educational ladder. All in all, there is only slight evidence of a proportionate increase in managerial positions of persons with lower social origins and this has been accomplished through education and the attainment of professional qualifications.

Of the higher reaches of the civil service, T. H. Farrer (Kelsall, 1955) had this to say in 1871:

> It selects men by a competitive examination, demanding an expensive education in high subjects in early years, which only the rich can afford. It offers no opportunity to those who cannot afford this early education, of afterwards making good their way.

In 1950, however, this situation had changed. Before World War II the children of manual workers made up less than 10% of those civil servants above the grade of Assistant Secretary, but in 1950 their contribution reached 17%; a small increase, perhaps, but the direction is up. Of those who entered the higher ranks of the civil service through promotion before the war, one-third originated from lower social strata (Registrar General's Classes III, IV and V), while in 1950 this proportion had increased to 40%. Even though Social Classes I and II still contribute most heavily to the higher ranks of the civil service, the chances of the children of manual workers to enter this elite have increased significantly during this century.

Changes in roads to the top

Perhaps the two most remarkable changes in the past hundred years have been in the complexity of technology and access to education. The public railway (1825), the Bessemer process for steel-making (1855–6), international telegraph cables (1866), public telephones (1877), automobiles (1886), the steam turbine (1889), power stations (1890), the astonishing advances in physics, chemistry and engineering, transistors and computers (Forbes and Dijksterhuis, 1963): the products of these changes had to be built, rebuilt, maintained and adapted to new uses. The circle of more markets requiring more goods which stimulated the search for even more markets was in full tilt. The World Wars produced more horrific and more complex weaponry, and the race to the moon or Mars or Venus continues to be one of the greatest stimuli to technological development. Concomitant with these technological changes came educational changes: compulsory attendance at elementary schools until thirteen years of age (1870), the raising of the school leaving age to fourteen in 1900, the creation of secondary schools, entrance to which poverty was not an insurmountable barrier (1902, 1907), the 1944 Education Act with its hope of secondary education for all and the elimination of social distinctions between academic and practical education, the abolition of fees in maintained and aided secondary schools in 1945 and now a school leaving age of sixteen, an official policy of comprehensive education and considerable controversy over the place of the public school in British society.

Education has become more and more important as a road to the top. Guttsman noted in his study of the British political elite that the professions were important avenues to the top for those who began in the middle and working classes and that more use was being made of the 'expert' in cabinet ranks. Clements told of an increased demand for graduates by the industrial firms he investigated. The recruitment of those who had left school under sixteen with no certificate and of those with slightly lower than top social origins and minor public school education who had previously attained their positions through some private and personal connection was declining. Education alone was not yet sufficient to assure the winning of the race to managerial levels but without it and without high social origins one could not enter even the starting line-up.

As noted earlier, there is some evidence that education is more important than social origins in the selection of marriage partners, although it should be borne in mind that achieved social status and education are very closely allied (Berent, in Glass, 1954).

> ... taking the group of marriages in which there is matching on education, a relatively substantial degree of discrepancy in social origin is possible, namely 53·9%. But in the group in which husband and wife have the same social origin, the degree of discrepancy in education is only 27·1%.

Education, rather than love, conquers all.

Changes in social differences

Depending upon the year which one takes as a basis for comparison, changes in living conditions are seen as more and less dramatic. In the case of infant mortality, for example, Dr. Holland, physician to the Sheffield General Infirmary, presented figures on numbers and causes of deaths for the period 1837 to 1842 (Thompson, 1963) which showed an infant mortality rate of 250 per 1,000 live births for age groups 0 to 1 and a rate of 506 per 1,000 live births for age groups 0 to 5. Compare these figures with those on page 46 and some idea will be gained of the improvement in general living conditions and health standards since the first half of the last century. Although infant mortality rates for all occupational groups have declined over time, it is still the case that infants in higher occupational groups have a better chance of surviving the first year of life, as can be seen in Figure 1 which shows the deaths of infants between the first four weeks and the first year of life (post-neonatal).

Mortality rates of occupational groups are still not the same but the differential amongst these groups has decreased. For example, estimates of the average age at death for gentry, tradesmen and labourers in 1842 (Thompson, 1963) according to the place of death show considerable gaps in physical life chances. For the gentry the age at death varied from 35 in Liverpool to 52 in Rutlandshire while for labourers it varied from 15 in Liverpool to 38 in Rutlandshire. As can be seen from

Figure 1

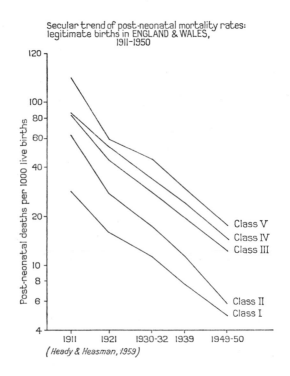

Secular trend of post-neonatal mortality rates: legitimate births in ENGLAND & WALES, 1911-1950

Post-neonatal deaths per 1000 live births

Class V
Class IV
Class III
Class II
Class I

(Heady & Heasman, 1959)

Figure 2, in this century the gaps have narrowed, but not closed. The expected occupational gradient may have been upset for the 1949–53 period by peculiarities in the classification of occupations (Susser and Watson, 1962).

Until the Booth (1892–97) and Rowntree (1901) surveys it was difficult to obtain a reasonably accurate picture of the differences in income amongst occupational groups. Even today, those classified as middle and upper middle class appear slightly reticent in revealing their total incomes to interviewers. An attempt was made by Dudley Baxter (Cole and Postgate, 1961) to estimate the differential distribution of income in 1867; however, his estimates covered less than half of those receiving incomes in England and Wales. Of the total, 79% (the working class) earned less than £100 per year while 0·5% (the upper and upper middle classes) earned from £1,000 to more than £5,000 per year. Between 1873 and 1896, due to a fall in prices and about a 5% increase in wages, employed, skilled men enjoyed a rise in real wages of about 35 to 40% (Cole and Postgate, 1961); profits and interests from industry and income from house property also rose. However the workers' share of the national income soon fell with the rising prices following 1900 (Cole and Postgate, 1961).

Wages were reckoned as having constituted in 1880 about 41 or 42% of the national income; in 1913 they were only 35 or 36%.

In 1946, wages, salaries and forces' pay accounted for two-thirds of the gross national product, the remaining third consisting of rents, interest and profits (Cole and Postgate, 1961). Higher taxation and other measures directed towards the levelling up of monetary standards have done much to lessen the income gaps amongst

Figure 2

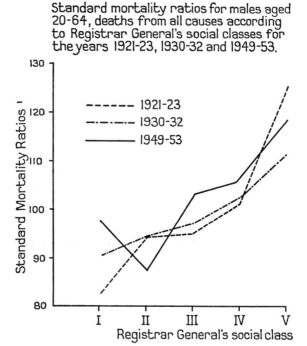

Standard mortality ratios for males aged 20-64, deaths from all causes according to Registrar General's social classes for the years 1921-23, 1930-32 and 1949-53.

------ 1921-23
—·—·—· 1930-32
———— 1949-53

[1]The standard mortality ratio is a measure of the difference between deaths in a given occupational group and deaths in a standard population consisting of all males in England and Wales aged 20–64. A ratio of 100 means that deaths within the age and occupational group follow the overall pattern for England and Wales; a ratio of less than 100 means that fewer than expected deaths occurred in that occupational group in relation to all males; a ratio of more than 100 means that more than expected deaths occurred in that occupational group in relation to all males.

occupational groups. Deliberate government intervention has done a great deal to erase much of man's inhumanity to man by providing the machinery by which a better than mere subsistence standard of living can be available to all.

The provision of free and compulsory elementary education dates from 1891 and free and compulsory secondary education from 1945, but coexisting with the state system is a private system and differential advantage still accrues to those who can use this private system. In 1907 a certain proportion of places in the secondary schools was made available free, to those considered able to benefit by such an education on the basis of an examination at 11 plus; but rather than decreasing the differential advantages of children from upper status categories, it was found that already advantaged children were six times more likely to obtain a free place than already disadvantaged children (Floud, in Glass, 1954). A real decrease in disadvantage occurred in the case of sons of either skilled manual or routine non-manual workers; the odds against their obtaining a secondary education fell from 12 to 1 in the case of those born in 1889 or earlier, to 4 to 1 for those born during the period 1920 to 1929 (Floud, in Glass, 1954). For those born in the late 1930's the differential has persisted; 62% of boys from status categories 1–3 (Hall-Jones), 20% from 4 and 5 and 10% from 6 and 7 obtained a grammar school type education (Little and Westergaard, 1964). One result of the 1944 Education Act was to increase the number of upper working class children in grammar schools (evidence for the Greater London area) but children of the lower working class were left considerably underrepresented in the grammar school population (Himmelweith, in Glass, 1954).

The expansion in the number of university places in the first four decades of this century has not as yet produced marked reductions in the differential opportunities for university education for status groups. Proportions of boys in status groups reaching university have increased in all cases of comparisons between those born before 1910 and those born during the period 1910 to 1929; the greatest percentage increase in boys from status categories 1 and 2, the least in boys from status categories 6 and 7 (Floud, in Glass, 1954). To some degree these figures are reflections of differences in access to secondary education, but a pattern of early leaving found more often amongst children of manual rather than non-manual workers is also contributory and it is not dependent upon levels of ability (Higher Education, 1963). It remains to be seen what changes in educational achievement the recent changes in educational policy will produce. Previous changes, while modifying slightly the circumstances of lower status groups, have benefited disproportionately the middle and upper status groups. Much of the difficulty lies not with an inequality of opportunity but with an inequality of access to opportunity—unequal chances of learning basic techniques and concepts which would enable a child to effectively compete for opportunities open to all who possess the qualifications.

For the working class one of the most important changes in family life over the last century has been the separation of home and work. The working class family today has ceased to be a single productive unit and now has some 'family life' which is distinct from activities involved in earning a living. For example, in the early nineteenth century a report from a Parliamentary Commission on women and factory work concluded that factory work was detrimental to family life. If a woman had learned any of the domestic arts, she had no time to practise them with the work schedule she had: up at five, work from six to eight, thirty minutes for breakfast, work from eight-thirty to twelve, one hour for dinner, work till seven. Children were taken along to the factory and put to work as soon as possible. The work pattern appropriate to rural conditions had been transferred to the city, and besides, the family needed the money. Factory Acts, Employment Acts and sanitation measures increased the possibilities for family life amongst the workers so that by the latter part of the nineteenth century working and living conditions for the ordinary people were better than before but still not 'good' (see, for example, Booth's monumental work on London life and labour).

After 1870 the size of middle and upper class families decreased fairly rapidly, but not until after World War I did smaller families become more characteristic of all classes. The proportion of manual workers using birth control methods increased by 17%, from 49% of those marrying before 1929 to 66% of those marrying during the period 1950 to 1960 (Klein, 1965).

The changing system of production, the compulsory education of children, the proliferation of occupations and the decreasing tendency for children to follow exactly in the occupational footsteps of fathers, the bombing, the building of new towns and the consequent physical separation of home and workplace: these factors were instrumental in breaking the working class family as a productive unit and making it a consumption unit as the middle class family. Other general trends in family relationships were summarized by Klein (1965), although she emphasized that some were based upon tenuous evidence. Changes seem to be

> ... from a close-knit family network to a more loose-knit one; from a community-centred existence to greater individuation ... to a more home-centred one ... to greater participation in associational life; from a segregated conjugal relationship to greater partnership in marriage; from traditional occupational choice to social mobility; ... from financial stringency to greater affluence; from emphasis on the breadwinner to emphasis on the child.

It would appear as if the traditional working class family were being released from the bonds of conformity to which it had been confined by economic necessity and social and cultural inheritance.

The loosening of traditional ties and more educational opportunities had not increased the chances of lower status groups to move to higher status groups at the time of the social mobility study carried out through the London School of Economics (Glass, 1954). Indeed, one of the main conclusions was that

> ... there have been no major differences between successive generations in the overall intensity of the status association between fathers and sons.

In a recent paper Yasuda (1964) doubted that this conclusion could be taken to mean that intergenerational mobility had not changed in the last half century; indeed, Glass prefaces his conclusion with 'according to our data'.

Changes in the shape of the occupational hierarchy

Although Karl Marx forecast the increasing misery of

86

the working class and its reduction to a homogeneous mass of individuals each doing the same kind of coarse, unskilled, monotonous work, four factors stand out concerning changes in the occupational structure: an increase in professional workers, a proportionate increase in clerical workers, increases in the ranks of skilled workers and a considerable *decrease* in unskilled and casual labour. For 1867 Dudley Baxter estimated that 23% of the total population were in the middle and upper classes, the rest in the manual class, half of which consisted of unskilled and agricultural workers, but when Sir Alexander Carr-Saunders and Professor Caradog Jones estimated the occupational distribution of occupied males (based upon the 1931 Census and calculated in terms of degree of skill), even allowing for differences in classification, the proportion of unskilled workers had dropped considerably (Cole, 1955). Because there were no studies on the grading of occupations before the research cited here, we cannot say much about any changes in the estimates of the social value of different occupations. However, Cole (1955) had noted that the new professions, accountancy, management, company directors and engineers had difficulty in claiming what was considered adequate social status and that frequently, social recognition was granted by members of the older professions and aristocracy only to leaders in the new professions. We have no idea of the social recognition granted by manual workers.

Changes in the number of strata

In the present state of our knowledge about social stratification in Britain, changes in the number of social strata seem to depend primarily on the kind of research being done. For example, national surveys have used five strata

(Registrar General's social classes), thirteen strata (Registrar General's socio-economic groups), seven strata (London School of Economics' mobility study); while studies of communities and cities have shown various numbers of strata. Margaret Stacey (1960) found that it was not possible to accommodate everyone in a class system in her study of Banbury, but that it was more meaningful to divide the population into a traditional class system and non-traditional status groups.

These differences are to be expected as different investigators look at different aspects of life, as people become more mobile and move into strange social surroundings and are unable to place new people into old categories. Only in rigidly stratified societies would one expect to find a single stratification system to which all in the society would agree and in which all would be accommodated. Even then, one's expectations could remain unfulfilled.

Changes in beliefs concerning social value

The writings of Tom Paine and the tenets of Methodism fired imaginations and goaded some radicals to action but the French Revolution inspired the British upper middle classes to action of their own; action oriented not to higher wages, better living conditions and political enfranchisement for the poor but rather to passive acceptance of their lot, quietism and discipline (Thompson, 1963).

> The message to be given to the labouring poor was simple and was summarized by Burke in the famine year of 1795: 'Patience, sobriety, frugality and religion, should be recommended to them; all the rest is downright fraud'.

This policy had some success as seen by the successful bribery of the Westminster electorate by servants of the Duke of Northumberland using beer and hunks of bread and cheese (Thompson, 1963). In the 1832 Reform Bill, to ensure that the vote would be used with 'sober consideration', only those workingmen who could pass muster under the £10 qualification stipulation were given the vote. The upper and middle classes granted concessions to workingmen in hopes of preventing the forcible seizure of more concessions rather than because of any significant change in their ideas about the social value of labour and of those who labour.

However, Liberals, Radicals, Trade Unionists and private individuals persisted in fighting and propagandizing for the 'rights of man' and in the application of these rights to the majority of the population. Chamberlain in 1885 published an 'unauthorized programme' in which he stated that private industry owed the community a ransom which it should be made to pay, to provide, for example,

... free education, good housing, fair rents ... Church disestablishment ... and the revision of the system of taxation. (Cole and Postgate, 1961).

The major political parties today are committed to social legislation and although the intensity of their commitments appears to wax and wane, social conscience is part of all party programmes.

Summary

In this necessarily brief introduction the selection of facets of social stratification has produced neglect of many important aspects. For example, most of the data has been derived from studies of white males so as not to introduce at this stage the complicating factors of sex and race. Absent also was any discussion about the relative advantages and disadvantages of various indices used to delineate social categories; nor have we considered at any length comparisons of Britain with other industrial societies. Apart from a few words here and there, the whole problem of the relationship between class, status and power groups has been omitted, as has the question of organized interest groups such as trade unions and employee and professional organizations in relation to the securing of advantages.

What we have shown is the pervasiveness of evaluation and its tenacity over time so that it would seem that although all changes, all stays the same. The general level of living for the majority of the population has altered almost beyond recognition in the last hundred years. The working man has been accepted as a citizen with full competing rights in the race for opportunities. What he still does not have is equal access in signing up for the race. Still prevalent is the idea of 'character' instilled either by high status parents or by the public school; but frequently it appears to be forgotten that such character has been instilled, as in the popular dictum, 'Leaders are born, not made'. Concern with equality and the definition of inequality as 'bad' arises only in those societies where there is a positive value attached to social equality. Such concern would be incomprehensible where inequality was considered to be 'good', 'just' and a 'natural state of affairs'; but in Britain, social equality is an official belief so that, at best, widespread social inequality can be considered incongruous.

In his address to the annual conference in 1948, the President of the National Association of Local Government Officers took notice of the official belief (Lockwood, 1958):

You and I . . . have been brought up in a world which recognized without question the social ascendancy of the white collar over the worker's muffler and its undisputed right to a preferential salary. Have we realized that that world has gone for ever . . .

How long is 'for ever'?

Suggestions for further reading

The literature on social stratification is considerable but the suggestions made below together with references cited in the bibliography are aimed at helping the student to locate those specific areas of the subject in which he is most interested.

BASCOM, W. R., 'Social Status, Wealth and Individual Differences Among the Yoruba', *American Anthropologist*, liii (1951), pp. 490–505.

BELLAH, R. N., *Tokugawa Religion*, Glencoe, Illinois: The Free Press, 1957.

BLOCH, M., *Feudal Society*, Vols. I and II, London: Routledge & Kegan Paul, 1962.

BOTTOMORE, T. B., *Classes in Modern Society*, London: Allen & Unwin, 1965.

BOTTOMORE, T. B., and RUBEL, M., *Karl Marx. Selected Writings*, London: Penguin Books.

BUCKLEY, W., 'On Equitable Inequality', *American Sociological Review*, xxviii (1963), pp. 799–801.

CENTRAL ADVISORY COUNCIL FOR EDUCATION, *Early Leaving*, London: H.M.S.O., 1951.

COULBORN, R., *Feudalism in History*, Princeton, N.J.: Princeton University Press, 1956.

Current Sociology, a U.N.E.S.C.O. publication. Two volumes in particular are immediately relevant: 'Social Stratification', ii,

No. 1, 1953–1954 and 'Social Stratification and Social Mobility: U.S.A., Sweden, Japan', ii, No. 4, 1953–1954.

DUBE, S. C., *Indian Village*, London: Routledge & Kegan Paul, 1955, and *India's Changing Villages*, Ithaca, N.Y.: Cornell University Press, 1958.

GENERAL REGISTRY OFFICE, The Census volumes, Mortality Tables and Classification of Occupations, London: H.M.S.O., various dates.

HOEBEL, E. A., JENNINGS, J. D., and SMITH, E. R., *Readings in Social Anthropology*, New York: McGraw-Hill, 1955.

HUACO, G. A., 'A Logical Analysis of the Davis-Moore Theory of Stratification', *American Sociological Review*, xxviii (1963), pp. 801–804.

International Bibliography of the Social Sciences, a U.N.E.S.C.O. publication.

MARX, K., and ENGELS, F., The German Ideology, Parts I and III, New York: International Publishers, 1939.

MAYER, K. B., *Classes and Society*, New York: Random House, 1955.

MILLS, C. W., *The Marxists*, New York: Dell Publishing, 1962.

MOORE, W. E., 'But Some are More Equal Than Others', *American Sociological Review*, xxviii (1963), pp. 13–18.

NADEL, S. F., *A Black Byzantium*, London: Oxford University Press, 1942.

SCHUMPETER, J. A., *Imperialism and Social Classes*, Oxford: Basil Blackwell, 1951.

SERVICE, E. R., *A Profile of Primitive Culture*, New York: Harper, 1958.

Sociological Abstracts, this journal contains abstracts of books and journal articles classified both by subject matter and by author.

SRINIVAS, M. N., et al., *Current Sociology*, 'Caste', viii (1959).

STINCHCOMBE, A. L., 'Some Empirical Consequences of the Davis-Moore Theory of Stratification', *American Sociological Review*, xxviii (1963), pp. 805–808.

THOMAS, G., *The Mobility of Labour in Great Britain, 1945–1949*, London: Central Office of Information, Social Survey Report 134, 1953.

TUMIN, M. M., 'On Inequality', *American Sociological Review*, xxviii (1963), pp. 19–26 (references to part of the continuing controversy over the Davis-Moore theory can be found as a footnote to this article).

WEBER, M., *The Theory of Social and Economic Organization*, London : Collier-Macmillan, 1964, especially chapters entitled 'The Types of Authority and Imperative Coordination' and 'Social Stratification and Class Structure'.

Bibliography

BARBER, B., (1957), *Social Stratification*, New York: Harcourt, Brace & World.

BENDIX, R., and LIPSET, S. M., (1953), *Class, Status and Power*, Glencoe, Illinois: Free Press.

BENE, E., (1959), 'Some Differences Between Middle-Class and Working-Class Boys in Their Attitudes Towards Education', *British Journal of Sociology*, x, pp. 148–152.

BERNSTEIN, B., (1958–1959), 'Some Sociological Determinants of Perception', *British Journal of Sociology*, ix, pp. 159–174; 'A Public Language: Some Sociological Implications of a Linguistic Form', *British Journal of Sociology*, x, pp. 311–326.

BOOTH, C., (1892–1897), *Life and Labour of the People in London*, London: Macmillan.

BOTT, E., (1957), *Family and Social Network*, London: Tavistock Publications .

CAPLOW, T., (1964), *The Sociology of Work*, New York: McGraw Hill.

CAUTER, T., and DOWNHAM, J. S., (1954), *The Communication of Ideas*, London: Chatto & Windus.

CENTRAL ADVISORY COUNCIL FOR EDUCATION, (1960), *15 to 18*, London: H.M.S.O.

CLEMENTS, R. V., (1958), *Managers: A Study of Their Careers in Industry*, London: Allen & Unwin.

COLE, G. D. H., (1955), *Studies in Class Structure*, London: Routledge & Kegan Paul.

COLE, G. D. H., and POSTGATE, R., (1961), *The Common People*, London: Methuen.

COPEMAN, G. H., (1955), *Leaders of British Industry*, London: Gee.

COSER, R. L., (1964), *The Family: Its Structure and Functions*, New York: St. Martin's Press.

DAVIS, K., (1949), *Human Society*, New York: Macmillan.

DAVIS, K., *and* MOORE, W. E., (1949), 'Some Principles of Stratification' in *Sociological Analysis*, L. Wilson and W. L. Kolb, New York: Harcourt, Brace.

DIEHL, C., (1923), 'The Government and Administration of the Byzantine Empire' in *The Cambridge Medieval History*, planned by J. B. Bury, London: Cambridge University Press.

DIEHL, C., (1957), *Byzantium: Greatness and Decline*, translated by N. Walford, New Brunswick, N.J.: Rutgers University Press.

DOUGLAS, J. W. B., and BLOMFIELD, J. M., (1958), *Children under Five*, London: Allen & Unwin.

DRUCKER, P., (1951), *The Northern and Central Nootkan Tribes*, Washington: Smithsonian Institution, Bureau of American Ethnology, no. 144.

FLOUD, J., HALSEY, A. H., and ANDERSON, C. A., (1961), *Education, Economy, and Society*, Glencoe, Illinois: The Free Press.

FORBES, R. J., and DIJKSTERHUIS, E. J., (1963), *A History of Science and Technology*, London: Penguin Books.

FORTES, M., and EVANS-PRITCHARD, E. E., (1948), *African Political Systems*, London: Oxford University Press.

GERTH, H. H. and MILLS, C. W., (1958), *From Max Weber: Essays in Sociology*, New York: Oxford University Press.

GITTUS, E., (1960), *Conurbations*, Unpublished Master's Thesis, University of Liverpool.

GLASS, D. V., editor, (1954), *Social Mobility in Britain*, London: Routledge & Kegan Paul.

GOLDTHORPE, J. H., and LOCKWOOD, D., (1963), 'Affluence and the British Class Structure', *Sociological Review*, xi, pp. 133–163.

GUSFIELD, J. R., and SCHWARTZ, M., (1963), 'The Meaning of Occupational Prestige: Reconsideration of the NORC Scale', *American Sociological Review*, xxviii, pp. 265–271.

GUTTSMAN, W. L., (1963), *The British Political Elite*, London: MacGibbon & Kee.

HALL, J., and JONES, D. C., (1950), 'Social Grading of Occupations', *British Journal of Sociology*, i, pp. 31–55.

HALSEY, A. H., and GARDNER, L., (1953), 'Selection for Secondary

Education and Achievement in Four Grammar Schools',
British Journal of Sociology, iv, pp. 60–75.

HARBURY, C. D., (1962), *Descriptive Economics*, London: Pitman.

HEADY, J. A., and HEASMAN, M. A., (1959), *Social and Biological Factors in Infant Mortality*, London: H.M.S.O.

HERSKOVITS, M. J., (1952), *Economic Anthropology*, New York: Alfred A. Knopf.

Higher Education, (1963), London: H.M.S.O.

HIMMELWEIT, H. T., HALSEY, A. H. and OPPENHEIM, A. N., (1952), 'The Views of Adolescents on Some Aspects of the Social Class Structure', *British Journal of Sociology*, iii, pp. 148–172.

HOLLINGSHEAD, A. B., and REDLICH, F. C., (1958), *Socal Class and Mental Illness: A Community Study*, New York: John Wiley.

HUTTON, J. H., (1946), *Caste in India*, London: Cambridge University Press.

JENKINS, D. C., JONES, E., HUGHES, T. J., and OWEN, T. M., (1960), *Welsh Rural Communities*, Cardiff: University of Wales Press.

KELSALL, R. K., (1955), *Higher Civil Servants in Britain*, London: Routledge & Kegan Paul.

KENNEDY, M. D., (1963), *A History of Japan*, London: Weidenfeld & Nicolson.

KLEIN, J., (1965), *Samples from English Cultures*, Vols. I and II, London: Routledge & Kegan Paul.

LITTLE, A., and WESTERGAARD, J., (1964), 'The Trend of Class Differentials in Educational Opportunity in England and Wales', *British Journal of Sociology*, xv, pp. 301–316.

LIPSET, S. M., and BENDIX, R., (1959), *Social Mobility in Industrial Society*, Berkeley and Los Angeles: University of California Press.

LOCKWOOD, D., (1958), *The Blackcoated Worker*, London: Allen & Unwin.

LOGAN, W. P. D., (1960), *Morbidity Statistics from General Practice*, London: H.M.S.O.

LURIA, A. R., (1960), 'Experimental Analysis of the Development of Voluntary Action in Children', *Perspectives in Personality Research*, H. P. David and J. C. Brengelmann, editors, New York: Springer.

LURIA, A. R., and YUDOVICH, F., (1959), *Speech and the Development of Mental Processes in the Child: An Experimental Investigation*, O. KOVASC and J. SIMON, translators, London: Staples.

M'GONIGLE, G. C., and KIRBY, J., (1936), *Poverty and Public Health*, London: Gollancz.

MAIR, L., (1962), *Primitive Government*, London: Penguin Books.

MALINOWSKI, B., (1948), 'Myth in Primitive Psychology', *Magic, Science and Religion and Other Essays*, Glencoe, Illinois: The Free Press.

MARSH, D. C., (1958), *The Changing Social Structure of England and Wales*, London: Routledge & Kegan Paul.

MARX, K., (1961), *Capital*, i, London: Lawrence & Wishart.

MARX, K., and ENGELS, F., (1934), *Manifesto of the Communist Party*, London: Martin Lawrence.

MINISTRY OF LABOUR, (1963), *Household Expenditure Survey*, London: H.M.S.O.

MYERS, J. K., and SCHAFFER, L., (1954), 'Social Stratification and Psychiatric Practice: A Study of an Out-Patient Clinic', *American Sociological Review*, xix, pp. 307–310.

NEWSON, J., and NEWSON, E., (1963), *Infant Care in an Urban Community*, London: Allen & Unwin.

PIERCE, R., (1961), 'The Extent of Family Planning in Britain', *Family Planning*, x.

REGISTRAR GENERAL, (1950), (1960), *Classification of Occupations*, London: H.M.S.O.

Registrar General's Decennial Supplement, (1958), England and Wales, Occupational Mortality, London: H.M.S.O.

ROBB, J. H., (1954), *Working-Class Anti-Semite*, London: Tavistock Publications.

ROWTREE, B. S., (1901), *Poverty: A Study of Town Life*, London: Macmillan.

Royal Commission On the Distribution of the Industrial Population, (1940), London: H.M.S.O.

RUNCIMAN, W. G., (1966), *Relative Deprivation and Social Justice*, London: Routledge & Kegan Paul.

SEARS, R. R., MACCOBY, E. E., and LEVIN, H., (1957), *Patterns of Child Rearing*, Evanston, Illinois: Row, Peterson.

SMELSER, N. J., and LIPSET, S. M., (1966), *Social Structure and Mobility in Economic Development*, Chicago: Aldine.

STACEY, M., (1960), *Tradition and Change*, London: Oxford University Press.

SUSSER, M. W., and WATSON, W., (1962), *Sociology in Medicine*, London: Oxford University Press.

THOMAS, G., 'The Mobility of Labour in Great Britain', (1953), *Occupational Psychology*, xxvii, pp. 215–220.

THOMPSON, E. P., (1963), *The Making of the English Working Class*, London: Gollancz.

TUMIN, M. M., with FELDMAN, A. S., (1961), *Social Class and Social Change in Puerto Rico*, Princeton, N.J.: Princeton University Press.

VEBLEN, T., (1953), *The Theory of the Leisure Class*, New York: Mentor.

WARNER, W. L., (1960), *Social Class in America*, New York: Harper & Row.

WARNER, W. L., and LUNT, P. S., (1942), *The Status System of a Modern Community*, Yankee City Series, Vol. II, New Haven: Yale University Press.

WITTFOGEL, K. A., (1957), *Oriental Despotism*, New Haven: Yale University Press.

WRONG, D. H., (1960), 'Class Fertility Differentials in England and Wales', *The Milbank Memorial Fund Quarterly*, xxxviii, pp. 37–47.

YASUDA, S., (1964), 'A Methodological Inquiry Into Social Mobility', *American Sociological Review*, xxix, pp. 16–23.

YOUNG, M., and WILLMOTT, P., (1956), 'Social Grading by Manual Workers', *British Journal of Sociology*, vii, pp. 337–345.

YOUNG, M., and WILLMOTT, P., (1957), *Family and Kinship in East London*, London: Routledge & Kegan Paul.